THE WINNING MIND

By Sebastian Coe

The Olympians (with N. Mason)
More Than a Game (with D. Teasdale, D. Wickham)
The Running Year – A Fitness Log and Diary (with P. Coe)
Running For Fitness (with P. Coe)
Running Free (with D. Miller)

THE WINNING MIND

What it takes to become a true champion

Sebastian Coe

headline
business plus

First published in 2009 by
HEADLINE PUBLISHING GROUP
First published in paperback in 2010 by
HEADLINE PUBLISHING GROUP

1

Cataloguing in Publication Data is available from the
British Library

ISBN 978 0 7553 1884 1

Typeset in Stone Serif by Avon DataSet Ltd,
Bidford on Avon, Warwickshire

Printed in the UK by CPI Mackays, Chatham, ME5 8TD

Headline's policy is to use papers that are natural, renewable and
recyclable products and made from wood grown in sustainable
forests. The logging and manufacturing processes are expected to
conform to the environmental regulations of the country of origin.

HEADLINE PUBLISHING GROUP
An Hachette UK Company
338 Euston Road
London NW1 3BH

www.headline.co.uk
www.hachette.co.uk

In memory of my father

CONTENTS

Introduction

THE ROAD TO GOLD

*'Ninety-five per cent of what it takes
to be a champion takes place away from
the track.'*

I am often asked what motivates me to succeed, and how I apply the skills I learned as a middle-distance runner to my roles in politics and business. The answers to the first question are a passion for the job in hand and a wish to be the best I can be; the answer to the second is that I apply them daily. There are many parallels between training for a major sporting competition, campaigning as a politician and bidding for a multi-million-pound contract. My wish in writing this book is to share the stories of my experiences in a way that I hope others will find useful too.

We are living through a time of dramatic change – in business, economics and politics – on a local and global scale. The general mood in recent months has oscillated between optimism and despair, sometimes on a daily basis, depending on whether the news is of imminent economic collapse or the possibility of national transformation, as instanced by the landmark election of President Barack Obama in the USA.

The reality is that the road to a successful outcome is rarely a straight one. In the case of an Olympic champion, it can mean decades of dedication, train-ing, personal achievements and sometimes failure, leading to a single career moment. For an entrepreneur or business manager there may be many smaller successes and a number of setbacks before the goal is achieved.

In the case of Obama, brilliant oratory skills and sheer hard graft paved his path to the White House, but the election result was also perceived by some as not just the culmination of a two-year campaign but also of a 200-year civil rights struggle. Of course, like all leaders, he is unproven until he has been in office for some time, but the truth is that the election result was of itself a great achievement and a sign of leadership success because he has inspired others to raise their game and to see what is possible. Effective leadership inspires hope as well as belief that success is achievable.

THE QUEST FOR EXCELLENCE

Inspirational leaders need to have a winning mentality in order to inspire respect. It is hard to trust in the leadership of someone who is half-hearted about their purpose, or only sporadic in focus or enthusiasm. Leaders inspire and excite others to want to be like them. They make it possible to believe that we can all optimise our gifts and achieve great things. They engender a quest for excellence and commitment among the team and the individuals within it, in that no one wants to let the side down.

Aiming for excellence is not so much about gratifying the ego (beating everyone else for the sake of it) as the desire to see how far you can get, how much you can do – to become the best you can be.

But there is rarely anything glamorous or direct about the path to achieving excellence. Even a sportsperson who makes early progress because they are blessed with natural talent can only get to the top of their profession – and stay there – as the result of putting in the time, effort and hard work. The building blocks of learning are important and each step helps to strengthen and inform the next. The inspiration to succeed will often have its roots in childhood – whether as a result of being well supported, or as a positive response to growing up in a challenging environment. The strongest influence in my early years and through-out my athletics career was undoubtedly my father, whose strength of character and focus was a driving force that shaped much of my determination to develop a winner's mind. He lived by many of the leadership ideals that are described in this book.

MY FATHER, MY COACH

Behind every successful athlete there is usually an exceptional and often anonymous coach. In my own case, my coach was not only exceptional, he was also my father. It was a unique and evolving relationship that took the rest of the sporting world, and the media in particular, a long time to understand.

'Coach' on the track, 'Dad' at home, Peter Coe was a remarkable and highly intelligent man. He trained originally as a mechanical engineer and was serving in the merchant navy when his ship was sunk during the

Second World War. He was among a handful of survivors. He was captured and was later to jump from a moving train en route to a prisoner of war camp. From occupied France, he walked – all night, every night – across all kinds of terrain, until he eventually reached Spain. There he was imprisoned before returning to England a year later. His wartime experiences had a profound impact on his attitude to life. His determination and focus were unshakable. He was a man who seemed to know no fear which was not always advantageous, particularly on one occasion when punching a Sunday tabloid journalist. However, the punch was executed by someone with an abiding love of the noble art.

He appreciated life and inspired respect amongst all who knew him. Part of his strength as an athletics coach was his engineer's instinct for understanding and honing performance and function. His approach to training was intelligent, incisive and rigorously forensic. It was also revolutionary. He challenged the accepted training norms of the time and had an immense influence on the development of middle-distance athletics. An exceptional and largely self-trained coach, his example was without doubt an inspiration, not only to me, but to many others.

The general convention when I started to train

seriously was that long-distance training was important not only for long-distance events, but critical in order to achieve results over short distances too. Coaches tended to be obsessed with mileage role models of the time, such as David Bedford (UK), Peter Snell (NZ) and Jim Ryun (USA). Although steady-state running over longer distances is an important part of the athlete's physiological jigsaw, it was not enough to break new ground over the middle distances of 800m and 1500m.

From an early age, my coach used very much faster tempo training over shorter distances, building up resistance to the type of fatigue generated in race conditions. Nevertheless, because of the times I was achieving, the general expectation amongst other parents and coaches was that I must be running some 60/70/100 miles per week.

I remember standing by the side of the athletics track on one occasion when one of the other fathers came up and said, 'You're killing him.' My dad just looked at the guy coldly and said, 'Yes, yes, I'm killing him – right the way to the top.'

'Stay true to your own path and don't allow yourself to be hindered by others' expectations or limitations.'

As a young boy, of course, that was not an entirely uncomfortable encounter to witness – but one of the lessons I learned and that I have taken with me over the years is that you have to learn to stand your ground. Courage and grit to do it your own way is a prerequisite. You also need people around you who are prepared to stand on that ground with you, if you are going to achieve your long-term goals. Anything less means that you are hindered by other people's expectations rather than being inspired by your own.

A FLEXIBLE APPROACH

Sports people at the top of their game tend, like entrepreneurs, to have something of a frontier mentality. They are bold and brave in what they do – and they are prepared to embrace new ideas. It is crucial to be flexible in approach if you are to have any chance of being the best in your profession.

I have noticed, in individual endeavours in particular, that the people who reach levels of excellence tend to be very imaginative in their approach. They are looking along the same road as everyone else, but they have the ability to see further down the road, and yet at the same time have the ability to focus on short-term goals as well. In athletics that may be literally when they are running round the track – but I also mean it in a more general sense. It is a critical skill for an effective leader to master. It is a matter of striking a balance between maintaining stability and knowing when to take a risk; knowing when to hold back and when to act.

Those with a winning mentality are often more prepared to listen to criticism and to do things in a new way – to break out of orthodoxies if they can see no obvious reason why it is necessary just to follow what the last person has done.

Of course, it can take courage to set yourself apart from the crowd. Choosing to do things differently can be mistaken for arrogance, but in reality, taking a new approach is often born simply of a compulsion to keep driving forwards.

A LONG-TERM VIEW

When I first started racing in cross-country at a local level, we found that I was winning races by almost one and a half minutes. That's quite a large time gap. My father was delighted. But being an engineer, he understood work load and the potential for stresses and strains. He had an instinctive understanding of the mechanics of the body that made him very aware of the importance of body maintenance, and he would always take the long-term view when planning my training.

His aim was to minimise the stress on my (then) young joints and reduce the long-term wear and tear on the body. His view was that until all my joints and ligaments had properly matured it was important not to wear the natural machinery any more than was strictly necessary. He had an excellent eye for good engineering, and my subsequent training routine was typical of his scientific approach. He saw it as his responsibility to protect and maintain the body, avoid overuse injury and deliver a fully rounded athlete in their twenties, who was both physically and mentally the equal of any competitor.

I can think of many examples of the level of detailed and original thinking that went into my training programme. We lived in Sheffield, which is surrounded by hills on all sides, and we would often run the roads in the beautiful Peak District. Stress on joints is at its greatest when running downhill, with gravity increasing compaction into the surface of the road. In order to minimise this effect, I would run to the top of the hills out of the valleys. To avoid long and unremitting downhill sections, my father would then drive me down to the bottom of the hill, so I was back on the flat and ready to run uphill again. In that way I was minimising the potential for injury and long-term wear and tear.

His understanding of the causes of injury and the possible long-term effect of training led to some unique approaches, though simple in concept. A road surface, particularly in countryside, is often quite cambered. So if you're running for five or ten miles on any one side of the camber you will tend to favour one leg over the other. He wanted to avoid this happening, so when I went road-running in the country, he made sure that I always ran down the middle of the road. (To this day I follow the same habit, which makes my children laugh when I go out jogging with them.) He would sometimes drive the car along behind me to protect me from any passing cars. It's fair to say that his concern with biomechanics was not always appreciated by irritated drivers.

There was a lot of that kind of thinking, much of it rooted in good common sense, and I've always been grateful that he was an exceptionally good engineer. Looking back, his was a pretty radical approach – not least because no one had done it that way before – although his techniques have been adopted by many coaches since.

In any profession it pays to regularly test and

question the effectiveness of established methodology and to plan ahead for the long game. There is no doubt that the long-distance aspect of my training stood me in good stead, just through the sheer continuity of what I think of as the 'bread and butter' years when we focused on building experience and developing the strong foundation stones of mental and physical strength and stamina.

By the time I was fifteen or sixteen years old, some of my runs were well over ten miles, in steep, undulating terrain. Once you've mastered that kind of training there is not much in life that you fear physically, because out of physical strength comes mental resilience. I always knew that everything I had done in training was much harder than anything I was going to face in a race.

'There is no template for success in life.'

My coach's approach taught me an important lesson: that there is no one template for success in life. However, there are traits that seem common to those who succeed and lead in a way that is respected in every field. These include characteristics such as imagination, tenacity, the ability to listen, intuition and intelligence. Equally important is the ability to focus and stay on track for as long as it takes, self-management, an element of charisma, a degree of talent and sheer personal courage.

Practical and professional skills are important too, as well as knowing when to consult and listen to experts in fields other than your own. A leader needs to know and appreciate the individual strengths and weaknesses of those on their team. The role is as much about keeping everyone motivated and committed to the overall goal as ensuring that there are fail-safe systems in place to ensure that project management runs smoothly. That is why it is vitally important to keep channels of communication open, so that problems can be owned or detected at an early stage.

During the course of my own career, I have been inspired by outstanding leaders and have also been in leadership roles myself, in several different professions. En route through my sport, I met many other world-class athletes who drove themselves hard and expected to deliver nothing less than their best. Their insights at a formative stage in my career were invaluable. As an elected Member of Parliament (for Falmouth and Camborne) and later as William Hague's Chief of Staff, I worked alongside some of the brightest minds in modern British politics. More recently, during my chairmanship of the Olympic bid and currently as Chair of LOCOG (the London Organising Committee of the Olympic Games and Paralympic Games), I have helped create a highly focused and dynamic team that has responsibility for delivering the London Games in 2012.

In every field there is the need for clear vision and strong leadership. There is a common belief that leaders are born, not made. I am not so sure about that. There is also every chance that a leader is shaped – by their environment, by their ambition, by their role models, by the support they are given as they progress through life and by sheer determination. Our aim must always be that there should be no limit to what an individual from any background can achieve with focus and application – provided they recognise and grab their opportunity with both hands.

In reality, we live in a world where not everyone has an equal opportunity to succeed – sometimes through no fault of their own and where latent talent is sadly left undeveloped. However, a determined attitude and bravery in developing new ways of doing things are always prerequisites for success – and those with a positive attitude and a hunger to surpass themselves are most likely to thrive. Though not without the planning, vision, patience and experience needed to deliver consistent results.

In writing this book, my ambitions are four-fold. Firstly, to talk about why, from my own experience, I believe that almost anything can be achieved by anyone, provided they have the motivation and drive and can visualise the end goal clearly enough. By that, I don't mean medals or honours, but the realisation of a dream. Secondly, to look at the importance of attitude and what makes a winning team. Thirdly, to consider why strong leadership is important and how it can inspire achievement. And, finally, why it is crucial to give the next generation the inspiration and the opportunities that will encourage them to challenge themselves.

Personal success does not need to result in public acclamation. Self-esteem comes from self-belief and striving to become the best we can be. Over the years that I have worked in sport, business and public life, I have met many people whose Herculean efforts have resulted in achievements that are worthy of recognition, but whose endeavours will never be recognised publicly. It is safe to say that large areas of our national life would be unrecognisable but for the hidden efforts of these people who, for no obvious recompense, provide the foundations for other people's high-profile achieve-ments. Sport is such a good example of this.

Success stems not only from the overall achievement, but from a profound connection with the project in hand, the professional relationships and support earned from others and the challenges that occur and are overcome along the way.

'Winning is never guaranteed.'

'The road to gold' is usually boulder-strewn and there are few short-cuts. It does not run in a straight line from the starting line to a successful finish; it may take unforeseen twists and turns over many years and will involve planning, hard graft, daily challenges, frequent setbacks and many small wins along the way. Every one of those moments of effort (or miles in my case) will take you closer to a winning position and to your ultimate goal. Along the road there are often defining moments that direct the choices we make for ourselves.

You don't always win from a winning position but you rarely win from a losing position. And you are far more likely to make your way to that winning position if you have the courage to learn from the mistakes that you make along the way. The chapters that follow will help to ensure that everything you do takes you closer to that position.

1

CREATING THE VISION

'I cannot overstate the importance of having a vision. It is what you cling to, for dear life, when the project is proving particularly difficult.'

Achieving goals and becoming the best – in any sport or profession – is about so much more than simply having a plan. It is about creating and realising a vision – having the belief and the trust that you, and those you work with, have the skills to make something happen that is unique and worth the time, effort and sheer hard work that is involved in achieving the outcome. Often that vision was inspired by events and influences from an early age.

My own background was ordinary, but supportive. We were a very close-knit family and my parents were keen to help all four of their children to excel. My father had an inner strength and focus that had been honed by experiences in his own life. My mother had an equanimity that may have stemmed in part from her Indian background, and an energy and vitality that led her to train as an actress before she married. They had the kinds of financial pressures and concerns that affect most families, and when my sister was accepted as a pupil at the Royal Ballet School I can remember them trying to figure out how on earth they could fund her attendance out of the family income.

'Sport is the hidden social worker in our communities.'

Their influence is one of the reasons I feel so passionately about wanting the development stemming from the 2012 Games to be a legacy for sport and culture in the UK that all children can benefit from in the future. Sport is the hidden social worker in our communities. It does so much more to help children from deprived communities than any government department or quango can achieve on its own.

My early career was deeply entrenched in the world

of sport. Athletics dominated my life from the age of twelve, through two Olympic Games and numerous other championship events until I retired from competitive sport in 1990. Inevitably, that period of my career is defined by the world records and medal moments that marked the successes.

My political career also featured 'big moments', for good or for bad, whether it was winning my seat in the constituency of Falmouth and Camborne, or losing my seat in the subsequent election, or working alongside William Hague in his 1997 leadership campaign.

More recently, there was an interesting cross-over between both worlds when I worked in sport and politics to win the privilege of hosting the Olympic and Paralympic Games in London in 2012.

The fields of politics, sport and business have many contrasts, but there are many parallels too. They are all highly competitive fields and tend to be described in terms of the extremes of 'winning and losing', 'success and failure'. They thrive on the discovery of talented newcomers, and need always to remain alert to the threat from established players who may 'up' their game or change their policy. The value system is similar too. Traditional qualities of integrity, clarity and enthusiasm earn respect on and off the field. Whereas cheating, blaming or complaining tend to be penalised or dismissed. Only the financial rewards are variable, in that success and recognition don't lead automatically to wealth creation.

Big moments are the ones that people remember, although in many ways it is the dozens of smaller moments that make up that win that are the more realistic measures of success. Not everyone will have medal moments. There are not enough medals to go around. But the process of training to win, taking part in a life-changing event, the sense of being a part of something momentous – those are things to be celebrated and shared, and those are the moments that influence and inspire others to take part and perhaps shape the future. Having a clear vision of what you want to achieve – and keeping that vision centre stage against all odds – will keep you on track when facing the inevitable obstacles along the way.

DEFINING MOMENTS

In 1968, I was a schoolboy growing up amidst the steel mills and coal mines of south Yorkshire. One memorable day, at the age of twelve, I was dragged into our school assembly hall, along with all the other children in our school, where we were seated in tidy rows of steel-framed canvas-backed chairs to watch an old-style black and white television set, placed on a trestle table on the stage. The experience was a novelty for many of us, and a revelation. A series of images flickered on the box in front of us, showing scenes from the Olympic Games in Mexico that had taken place sometime the night before. We were there to watch two athletes from our own home city of Sheffield. Their names were John and Sheila Sherwood, and they were to redefine the course of my life from that day onwards. John was a hurdler. He won the bronze medal in the 400m hurdles that day. It was the memorable race in which David Hemery won Olympic gold and in doing so set a new world record. David Coleman, the BBC television commentator, said, in his inimitable style, 'Hemery first, [Gerhard] Hennige second, and who cares who came third.' Well, there were about a million of us in Sheffield who cared a lot on that day. And we cared, too, that his wife Sheila narrowly missed out on a gold medal to win silver in the long jump. David still smiles at his *faux pas* today.

> *'Each of us will experience moments*
> *in life that genuinely change the way*
> *we view the world.'*

There are moments in each of our lives when we experience something that genuinely changes the way we think about things: a painting or a piece of music, watching a sporting victory, or understanding something that is said or written. Watching that defining moment in local history was my moment of insight and change. I don't need to be told about the power of television, or the impact that seeing something at an early age might have on the future direction of a young life. I couldn't articulate my emotion in any defined way at the time. I just knew that I wanted to be a part of what I'd seen on that television screen that day.

Two weeks later, when John and Sheila returned home to Hillsborough running track, only a short distance from Sheffield Wednesday's football ground, I stood for over two and a half hours, waiting to catch a glimpse of the returning heroes as they walked past with their medals. Such was the impact of that experience that, shortly after, I joined the local athletics club. And when I was fourteen, it was Sheila who gave me a new pair of track shoes to take to my first English schools championships – at Crystal Palace.

Twelve years later, in 1980, I was representing Great Britain alongside Steve Ovett and others in the Moscow Olympic Games. For all of us it was to be a record-breaking and memorable Games. My personal journey from a school assembly hall in Sheffield to an Olympic arena in Moscow was, by any stretch of the imagination, a long apprenticeship – and a deeply challenging one – no different from the experience of many other athletes. And it had been ignited by the impact of what I'd seen on that television.

The memory of that moment of inspiration reminds me that every thought and action has the power to make an impact, on those around us and on what we may eventually become. The decisions we take each day will affect future generations. At the time of writing, there are still a few years to go until the 2012 Games. Many of the future competitors are still at school. At a time when our culture has become preoccupied with the trappings of fame and ways to achieve instant 'celebrity' status, there is a widespread and false expectation that success comes easily, or that media recognition is in itself the prize. In reality, nothing could be further from the truth. We owe it to the next generation to inspire them to take the long and often challenging 'road to gold', rather than the short-cuts to fame (which is often transient), in whatever field they choose.

WHO DARES WINS

Big moments in sport change lives: not only the lives of those achieving glory, but the lives of those watching as well. Just as watching the 1968 Olympics influenced my own destiny, so too there will be children heading for the nearest go-kart track in the wake of Lewis Hamilton's Formula 1 success, and children who are taking cycling and swimming a lot more seriously having watched Chris Hoy, Bradley Wiggins, Rebecca Adlington, Ellie Simmons, Dave Roberts and the rest of the British team bring home a cluster of gold medals from the Beijing Olympic and Paralympic Games. My hope is that these events will influence, in a positive way, where they find themselves in twenty years from now. Those who have trained to compete in a public event such as the annual London Marathon will already know that the discipline of training can enrich every area of life.

We all need heroes – but children need them more than most. Personalities from sport, TV and films have inspired and enthused children of every generation, and those who reach the top of their profession having made their way up from unexceptional backgrounds are the ones who offer the greatest evidence for others to see that 'Yes. I can do that too'.

Interestingly, there is now a new breed of hero on the block: entrepreneurs and business people. Television has had its part to play in this development, as a plethora of shows has turned a handful of wealthy, self-made entrepreneurs, often from modest backgrounds, into household names. Television programmes such as *The Apprentice*, *Dragons' Den* and *The Secret Millionaire* may not show the most rounded and positive side of business, but they have demystified some elements of how business operates and show that, in theory, 'anyone can do it'. Contestants appear in many ways to be little different from our next-door neighbours, which means that today's young people are more likely to see that entrepreneurial success is possible for them too. It has become more reasonable to aspire to being the next Richard Reed of Innocent or to follow in the footsteps of Dominic McVey, who, at the age of fifteen, developed a successful and highly profitable business selling and distributing micro-scooters via his home computer.

Even twenty years ago, only the most media-friendly of business entrepreneurs would be commonly known or would make popular media headlines, among them figures such as Anita Roddick, who created Body Shop, Richard Branson, founder of the Virgin empire, and historic figures such as Henry Ford or Andrew Carnegie. Revolutionaries and trailblazers one and all.

The Internet, the mobile phone and speed of access to information and communication means that things can move fast and deals can be done quickly. In one generation we have leapt from using limited to limitless technology. And in spite of, or perhaps because of, the recent economic downturn, the acquisition of wealth is increasingly attractive in its own right. But as most people come to realise, there is more to life than wealth creation, even in the business world.

STRIVE FOR SUCCESS: BUT NOT AT ANY PRICE

My own vision is not, and has never been, one of success for its own sake. Success for its own sake can also mean success at any price. In the world of sport that can lead to the use of performance-enhancing drugs, and in the business world it can lead, occasionally, to creative manipulation of the markets.

Having a clear set of values is therefore of paramount importance. High-profile moments of great achievement can and do inspire but equally Ben Johnson's big public moment in faking a dope test after having won the Olympic 100m title in 1988, for example, damaged the integrity of the sport. Evidence shows that it impacted Canadian track and field for the following decade and alienated young talent that would have otherwise become involved in the sport.

An interesting example of someone who is aware of the balance to be struck between creating and bestowing wealth is modern-day philanthropist Bill Gates, who, not content with transforming the world's technology through the international success of Microsoft, the company he founded, is now channelling billions of dollars to help thousands of disadvantaged people around the world via the Bill and Melinda Gates Foundation. Their declaration that 'All lives have equal value' is a clear statement of their vision. His example has influenced innumerable others who want to reconcile personal success with their desire to make a difference and to give something back. The greatest medal moments are not necessarily related to personal gain.

I cannot overstate the importance of having a vision. It is what you cling to, for dear life, when the project is proving particularly difficult – and that is probably the most important reason to have that vision, and the greatest motivator of all. A vision is not the same as a mission statement. A mission statement is simply a statement of intent and often merely restates the obvious; whereas a vision is intended to inspire people. A vision describes the landscape that you are helping people to navigate. It is bold, it is optimistic, it is often pioneering – and usually intensely personal. Although to get as far as you wish to go in any profession, particularly at a young age, usually requires a deeper level of passion and commitment than can be achieved by just one person.

For those who say they don't have a vision or a driving passion, I would say, revisit the here and now. What motivates you to get out of bed in the morning? What makes you feel driven to succeed? What do you want to be remembered for? What do you want to achieve? A vision is not an abstract concept without foundation. It has its roots in the present. It is an essential part of the master plan, the highest point of achievement that you can envisage for yourself and your team. It is a motivator and a way of encouraging one hundred per cent engagement. A leader without a vision and belief in that vision will find it more difficult to deliver, or to encourage others to engage in the process of delivery.

FROM VISION TO REALITY

*'I don't want this to come as a shock to you,
but you are going to an Olympic Games.'*

It was my father's voice, and I will always remember the moment I heard his words. We had been training for a couple of hours on a filthy night in Sheffield. I was completely soaked, shivering with cold, and the area that I had been training on was now more mud than grass. I had run several series of laps and completed a range of other exercises. I was ready to go home, get dry and join my brother and sisters for dinner. He threw me a tracksuit to put on for warmth and, as I walked up to the house, he said, almost as a throwaway line, 'Look, I've been thinking about this. I don't want this to come as a shock to you, but you will be going to an Olympic Games and I think we should start thinking about that now, because I've seen others melt under the pressure.'

I was fourteen years old.

When my father rekindled that seed of Olympic ambition in my mind, he did not do it to put undue pressure on me or to alarm me, but to hone the vision and start to plan for the reality. He could see the potential in what we had achieved over several months to that point, and he wanted to see whether the idea would inspire me and – importantly – allow me time to get used to the concept.

And I thought, with typical fourteen-year-old sangfroid, 'Oh yeah, right. Okay, fine.'

Looking back at my athletics career, it would be reasonable to ask, 'How on earth did you get here from there?' The answer is: steadily, and with a lot of planning and hard work. I started competing at school when I was twelve years old and was initially put forward for a west of Sheffield, schools championship. I then qualified to compete in the city championship and then a year later at South Yorkshire level and then on to county level, northern county and national level. At the time my father mentioned the Olympics, I was Yorkshire schools cross-country champion and was progressing to northern county level. He had recognised the possibility that the Olympics could be a genuine longer-term goal.

Aged fifteen and sixteen I won national youth titles and at eighteen a junior title. Each of those levels is a major goal in its own right, and within each of those goals is a series of smaller targets. At senior national level, the European Championships and Olympic Games become a potential reality. I competed in my first Olympic Games when I was twenty-three years old.

That was my route – but it is not the only one. Some athletes will come into the sport later.

In politics, instead of starting at first base and beginning my career by sitting on a council, I began my second career as an elected MP. Prior to that time I was only a member of the Party, but that didn't stop me knowing what I wanted to do. I had the benefit of valuable experiences in other arenas, including a useful period of time at the UK Sports Council (see page 109) and the Health Education Authority.

The very nature of settling upon a vision means that the compulsion to be driven by it remains strong. But your aspirations need to be shared with other people who can help make it happen. You need to communicate the vision and engage the imagination of those you want to bring with you – to show the people you work with that this is not just a vision for you, it's a vision they can believe in and be a part of as well. That was proven to me again and again throughout my athletics career and, later, during my time as a Member of Parliament, but perhaps never more so than when chairing the London bid to host the 2012 Olympic and Paralympic Games.

LONDON IN THE RUNNING

I became chairman of the Olympic bid on 19 May 2004, picking up the baton from Barbara Cassani, who had begun the process in 2002. She had already put in place an infrastructure and a team of talented people ready to take the bid forward, but at that stage the outcome was less than certain.

There were nine runners and riders at the start of the bidding process: London, Paris, New York, Madrid, Moscow, Havana, Istanbul, Leipzig and Rio de Janeiro. The IOC (International Olympic Committee) had dubbed it 'The Great Race' – and, in fairness, it was. But the initial evaluation of London's suitability as a host city had not been kind.

Our immediate job was to change the perception, both within and outside the bid team, that there were no pre-ordained reasons why we were destined to fail again just because our attempts to land the prize had been unsuccessful in the past.

We needed to show confidence and purpose to the electorate and the IOC, as well as to our stakeholders, to international sport, to domestic and international media and, crucially, to the public at home. We needed to show them that we had the best team in the field, that we knew what we were doing and that we were driven by a vision to transform the lives of young people.

WINNING HEARTS AND MINDS

Unless you can influence and inspire others to buy into and share your vision, you will not succeed. Success is possible only if each individual involved in the race understands the unique part they play in achieving the eventual outcome. When I was out there on the track, I was inspired to win not only for myself, but also for my coach, my backroom team, my family, my friends and, ultimately, my country. The same is true, to varying degrees, in all walks of life and in everything we do – and is never more important than when inspiring the next generation – our sporting heroes and leaders of tomorrow.

But you can't inspire people simply by barking orders from the touchline. You can't inspire people unless you first understand them. Delivering extraordinary speeches won't work unless you are clear in your own mind why you're giving those speeches. Nor is it enough to put together a team of people to win a tournament or a business contract unless you understand what motivates them and why they want to be part of the project.

So I asked myself and the members of the team, '*Why* do you want to do this? Why is it you're prepared to work tirelessly, seven days a week; to work more hours per day than in any organisation you have ever worked for; to allow weekdays and weekends to meld into one; to join an organisation with no certainty of outcome?'

Settling upon the vision is never a cursory or flippant process. It is not the same as devising a mission statement. The inhibitor to progress is often moving into the detailed project management without having a clear and compelling vision to help underpin and map the journey. In our case, it took many days to agree what the vision was.

Our bid was about the desire to make a difference to millions of children in the UK and around the world. It was a message that held enormous power in its simplicity and one that everybody involved fully committed to.

Once we were able to articulate the vision within our own teams, we were able to communicate our message with much more confidence. The media were crucial. With the media generally supportive, we were able to gain traction with the public locally, nationally and internationally. We were also able to explain to our families why they weren't going to see much of us for the next two years, why friendships and social lives had to be put on the back burner. That's what our teams bought into.

There were just sixty of us involved at the time, and it was the team who would go on to win the bid for London in Singapore on 6 July 2005. At the time of writing, the team is over 300 strong. And the central vision remains fixed. It is important that the bigger picture remains central to what we are planning to achieve.

One of the important roles of a leader in any situation is to lead by example. If the person who is leading the project has total faith in their team and total belief in the outcome of the project, it will be much easier for everyone else to commit themselves to making it happen too. By showing personal commitment to your goals you encourage others to feel committed also.

Developing self-discipline and dedicating yourself to hard work sound like tough and old-fashioned choices – particularly when we are living in an age of instant gratification. However, others on your team will be inspired to follow your example and the eventual trade-off is enormous. If each individual shares a common vision and understands the underlying values and principles of the company, brand or project, the team will be stronger because of it and will deliver more effectively.

THE IMPORTANCE OF 'WHY?' AND 'HOW?'

Project managers in any organisation will spend a lot of time drilling into two basic questions:

'*How* are we going to do it?'
'*Why* are we going to do it?'

But the questions are usually asked in the wrong order. It is impossible to decide *how* to do something effectively unless you can get to the heart of *why* you're doing it. It is the most important question to ask any individual or team before they start project planning.

Often, when people are asked 'why', they will start to explain the 'how' instead: *how* they did it last time; *how* they are going to achieve it this time; or what it will achieve; or, even worse, they will simply say, 'That's the way we've always done it.'

> *'"How?" and "Why?" are important questions that need to be asked in the right order.'*

There's nothing wrong with having a protocol, or doing something in a way that follows a set procedure along a proven path – in fact, it's essential once a project is underway. But unless there is commitment to a shared vision from the outset, there is a danger that what you are really developing is a number of separate projects with contrasting ideas about what the priorities are and what you are trying to achieve.

The vision that I wanted everyone to carry, with great clarity, in their minds and their hearts was quite simple and the core elements are relevant to any major project:

- If we keep emotional connectivity at the centre of what it is we are trying to achieve, then we will create emotional appeal
- If we keep personal responsibility at the centre of our objectives, then we will not want to risk letting anyone down
- If we keep young people at the centre, then we will remember that the 2012 Games (or the business you are involved in, or the hospital you are working in, or the school you are teaching in) has the potential to change and enhance the lives of future generations, in our case primarily through sport

It was a vision born of my own experiences in sport, but it was one that every single person on that team could relate to. Thankfully, when we made our presentation in

Singapore, the general public and the IOC bought into the vision too.

Success born of personal commitment is a passport to self-belief and increased self-esteem that reinforces the characteristics of the winning mind. And the potential for winning is often increased if more people share and are committed to the same vision.

2

SETTING THE GOALS

'Every goal is made up of a series of smaller, achievable steps that can eventually take you as high as you can envisage yourself wanting to go.'

A vision is an abstract concept. In order to turn a vision into reality there needs to be a plan of action, broken down into a series of achievable goals. There is nothing new or particularly insightful in that statement, but to succeed you need to be rigorous in the setting and achieving of those goals – and to make sure you maintain momentum and stay on track.

GOALS

Setting goals is vitally important, but they need to be appropriate goals. A consistent and single-minded approach to reaching short-term goals is often a more reliable way of achieving long-term success than a wealth of natural talent on its own.

Throughout my athletics career, the overall goal was always to be a better athlete than I was at that moment – whether next week, next month or next year. The object was always to improve – gradually, steadily, sustainably – and in achievable stages. The improvement was the goal. The medal was simply the ultimate reward for achieving that goal. It's an approach that I still apply now, in all aspects of my life.

When my coach said to me, with typical understatement, 'I think we need to start planning for the Olympics', he did not say it lightly. Few in their early teens have the self-awareness to be able to take the long-term view of their needs; they don't always see over the brow of the next hill. A good coach, like any good leader, needs to fire the imagination, to paint a picture of what might be there, where for some only a blank canvas exists. My coach wanted that picture to become so familiar that it became part of who we were and what we expected to achieve.

However, a talented schoolboy does not become a world-class athlete automatically, any more than a gifted entrepreneur becomes a millionaire immediately after launching their first idea. It can happen, of course, but rarely. My coach knew all too well that lasting success doesn't happen overnight.

He knew of athletes who had not focused on the vision of sustainable improvement leading to Olympic success early enough in their career. That lack of familiarity had meant that either they became overwhelmed by the enormity of the goal or they had not begun planning vigorously enough for it at an early enough stage. He knew that steady progress results from maintaining a consistent approach, trial and error, going back to 'first principles', hard graft, examining form and process and taking care to assess and correct any mistakes along the way.

I can say from personal experience that Olympic success was of less immediate importance in those early days than sheer curiosity and the personal challenge. How far *could* I go? What *might* I be able to achieve? From district level sports events onwards.

The same is true in most walks of life. Once you have captured the vision, it is important to focus thoughts and actions to keep yourself on track. Visualisation techniques are a powerful tool used by many people in professional sport as well as in business. If you assume that you are going to achieve your goals, and you can visualise yourself achieving them, you are far more likely to do everything you can to reach them. And since every goal is made up of a series of smaller steps, it makes sense to keep on going and to aim as high as you can. If you're inquisitive enough, that self-exploration will take you inevitably to a logical conclusion. If you want to explore far enough, why not envisage yourself getting right up to the point where someone puts an Olympic medal round your neck?

MEASURING PROGRESS

Of course, had my coach told me when I first started running competitively that my apprenticeship would take eleven years to complete, I might have found it daunting. Instead – with the help of *Athletics Weekly*, the essential reference for all track and field athletes at the time – he studied performance statistics and researched and set a series of times for me to achieve each year. (I have no doubt that he was also keeping an eye on the performance of one Steve Ovett, who was a year older than me and already making his mark.) The performance targets set by my coach were calculated to keep me on track for potential Olympic selection, and to provide a measure to keep us aware of how my performance compared to those of my potential competitors. As a result of his careful goal-setting, I met and exceeded those target times every year – apart from one, when I was injured.

I am focusing on this as a way of showing that large goals can only be achieved if they are strived for in a consistent manner. It is important to be able to measure progress in a realistic way, so that adjustments can be made if necessary, and that when assessing the competition you are making grounded and realistic judgements, rather than being solely emotional and instinctive.

I progressed steadily and stage by stage, from local to regional and eventually national schools level, before winning a Yorkshire county title. So by the time I won the English schools title, which nominally marked me out as being the best sixteen-year-old in the country, I was starting to realise that the Olympics, although realistically years away, was a part of the landscape.

STEVE OVETT

Generally speaking, when describing 'the competition' the phrase encompasses everyone or everything in your field; but sometimes, when you are at the top of your game, the field narrows, and it becomes more personal. You become aware that whenever you are aiming for the top slot, there is a single company or person who recurs as your main competitor.

The competitor who dominated most of my athletics career was Steve Ovett. I first became aware of him in the early 70s when he was winning the 400 and 800m races, and I was focusing on 3000m and cross-country distances. He was already featuring large in *Athletics Weekly*. Ovett had even featured on the cover, which was a landmark for an athlete.

My first experience of racing against Steve was in 1972 in the English schools' cross-country champion-ship in Hillingdon. An athlete called Kirk Dumpleton won first place; Steve finished second, and I finished ninth. I subsequently trained with Kirk Dumpleton when I was at Loughborough University, and he has since become known as the first of only a few athletes ever to have beaten both of us in the same race.

Steve would have been running for Sussex schools at the time. I would have been a year younger: pretty happy with my placing; but nonetheless aware of him as a winning talent. Steve was en route to winning silver in the 800m in the 1974 European Championships in Rome while I was still making my way through the youth and the junior ranks. By the time he was 18 and I was 17, he was everywhere and although we hadn't raced each other again since 1972, it was very clear to me that our paths were slowly converging.

CREATING A SUPPORT NETWORK

A clearly defined vision is essential to every success, but it is only part of the story. Goals are rarely set or met by one person on their own. When you see a sporting champion cross the finishing line, you don't see all the people who have helped them to arrive at that point. Behind the scenes of every achievement – in sport, politics, commerce or any other field of endeavour – are other people who have contributed to that success in different ways, not least by breaking the task into smaller, achievable goals and providing the support and belief that they will succeed.

I trusted my coach absolutely, and my achievements on the track were very much the result of our partnership and the involvement of our extended support team

– a physiotherapist, medical support and others who helped to sharpen my on-track performance over many years. My coach taught me how important it is for young people to have someone behind them from an early age, who can help map their route ahead and encourage and help them to achieve their potential. Leaders and managers in corporations have a similarly important responsibility. Winning minds are created from that kind of support and vision and mentoring, as many leaders of industry will verify.

THE IMPORTANCE OF PLANNING

Just as anchoring the vision is all about identifying and cementing the 'why' of the matter, so developing a plan of action is all about focusing on the 'how'. In many ways, outlining the vision of what you want to achieve and spurring people into action is the easy part. The vision engages the imagination and motivates people to want to become involved, but the success of any project depends upon careful planning and preparation.

'The "why" is the vision that motivates
people to succeed.

The "how" are the goals that are practical
and time-bound.'

The process of planning and early attention to detail help to engage people and encourage them to take ownership of their area of responsibility. Each team and each individual needs to be inspired to make their own contribution to the success of the project. Ultimately, the quality of the planning defines the quality of the outcome and overall success of any endeavour.

There are two factors involved in planning and delivering any major project – especially one like London 2012, which is one of the most complex pieces of project management any city can undertake:

- Broad strategic direction
- Tactical delivery

There is no doubt that having the right people in place from the outset to deliver the results you need is critical to overall success. This may sound an obvious statement, but it is vitally important that the people on the management team can be relied upon to operate in a coherent and cooperative way, with complementary skills and with an equal commitment to high-quality and effective project delivery. This is especially important when project delivery is a many-staged process and each stage is dependent upon the timely delivery of the stage preceding it.

My own approach to planning is collaborative and takes place over several stages. I trust my team to be far more expert than me in their respective disciplines, as I did with my backroom athletics team.

'A strong leader will always try to hire people who are brighter and have more potential than themselves.'

I tend to find that when you are focused on a great project, there is no need to go to work in the morning thinking that people need motivation. They are already motivated. Much of the time, the battle is actually suggesting, gently, that people might want to go home at 8 o'clock at night.

However, different people have different drivers. Everyone may be committed to the common goal, but they will be on different rates of pay, with different roles and responsibilities, and have different home commitments. An effective leader bears those variables in mind and wherever possible takes account of those individual differences.

It is important to value and nurture working

relationships. People who want to be inspired will raise their game to meet the demands of the task in hand if given the opportunity and the support to do so, but one of the greatest challenges for anyone in a position of leadership is to keep people motivated and on track through the more challenging times; to help maintain momentum, step by step, whilst also having the awareness and intuition to know when things are not going as well as they should be; and to anticipate who or what might undermine success in the longer term. A project-management system may flag up a potential difficulty, but it is often harder to get to the bottom of the real cause of that problem. In my experience, the greatest things are achieved by those who work together closely and who know each other well, because there is a greater understanding of strengths, weaknesses and common purpose. It can take years to fine-tune those working relationships. For example, my PA Susie Black has been a colleague since our time in William Hague's office.

But short-term working relationships can evolve fast and efficiently too when all parties are working towards the same goal. I worked closely with Ken Livingstone, Boris Johnson's predecessor as Mayor of London, during the preparation for the Olympic bid. On paper it was an unlikely partnership that crossed the political divide, but it worked very well because we shared a goal – and often a sense of humour, as I have also done with Boris Johnson.

PERSONAL STYLE

Anyone in a position of influence needs to be able to manage their own actions as well as leading the actions of others, and as such needs to have a realistic idea of their own strengths and weaknesses. It is important to recognise when other people's skills are needed as well as your own, when it is time to say, 'I can't take you any further with this', rather than saying, 'I'm going to *try* to turn myself into that kind of person'.

My own career has been lived out in the public eye. I am comfortable speaking in public and (as far as you ever can) I have an understanding of how the media operates. I have also been involved in the world of international sport for most of my adult life. All of which is useful when it comes to winning sponsorship support and gaining public support for the Olympics. On the other hand, I am less experienced in other functional and operational areas.

The chairman of any company needs to ensure they are always well briefed – no matter how tough or unpalatable that briefing may be. It is important to be able to provide an accurate and honest picture to private stakeholders or government bodies, with no room for surprises at a later date.

An effective team, especially one that is growing rapidly, needs to keep communicating and to ensure that decisions are taken at the appropriate level of control. The key is to ensure that strategic decisions and problems are discussed at board level, whereas functional decisions and processes are driven by the divisional heads. Problems tend to develop if those operating at a strategic level become too involved in the detail, or vice versa. This is true in any field – including sport: though it is important that all parties develop awareness and an understanding of each others' skills and priorities. For example, during my athletics career, my coach took strategic control of my training, and pulled everything together centrally, whereas David Martin, the physiologist, focused on the granular detail of the physiological components of my performance. My coach of course still needed a sufficient understanding of David's craft and its relevance to be able to plan the strategy accordingly.

A MATTER OF TIME

Time and expertise are two of the most important assets you can give any organisation – and to achieve a successful outcome they need to be managed effectively from the outset. Time management is not just about watching the clock and managing workflow; it also involves setting the pace and the momentum of the project.

In sport, perhaps more than any other field, every second can count and can mean the difference between winning and losing. You become very aware of the importance of time and how quickly it passes – not just in terms of track speed, but of age-related achievement as well.

'The project manager sets the pace, monitors progress and tunes in to the rest of the team.'

On the athletics track, the person who is setting the pace dictates the behaviour and the responses of the others alongside him or her. The same is true of project management. If a project is to be a success, the project manager will set the pace, monitor progress and tune in to the traits and behaviours of others on the team.

The more complex the project, the more important

it is to ensure that the project management system is sophisticated enough to flag what is on target and what is going off the rails.

The reality is that the vast majority of tasks that are scheduled should never come to the attention of senior management because they are planned and executed efficiently, effectively and on time by the team. It is only a select handful that should take up management time.

COMMUNICATION IS VITAL

'Leaders need to listen not only to what is being said, but also what is not being said.'

There are as many styles of management as there are people. I am not a great fan of desks and offices and so I tend to walk around and talk to people. I find it a very useful way of getting to know people and finding out what is really going on, listening for the questions that should be asked but are not. Keeping the lines of daily communication open and effective is absolutely crucial. Politically, this means taking time not just to speak with party members in conclaves but to listen to politically divergent views in the local supermarket. A good leader doesn't only listen to what is being said – they are intuitively tuned in to the sub-text as well. It is one of the most important aspects of leading a team.

The most important element of all in ensuring that any project will succeed is effective communication: up and down, formal and informal, always open, always honest. A combination of well-managed meetings and effective systems to support them is essential.

I see my role as very much about raising awareness, reminding people of the importance of what we are involved in and making them feel valued. It's important that on occasions I am seen out there at the front, defending when necessary and not hiding from reasonable debate and scrutiny, as well as picking the battles, often ones that are small enough to win and big enough to matter.

One of the greatest challenges of any leader is recognising when personal involvement is necessary and when it is more appropriate and more effective to lend support to others instead.

> *'You need to know when to lead from the front and when giving your support to someone else will be more effective.'*

There is often a transition from leading, to supporting, to letting go that enables the individual to grow in competence without becoming too dependent on the reassurance or support of others.

ALWAYS EXPECT THE UNEXPECTED

One of the most important elements when planning a project is always to anticipate the unexpected. You have to have a contingency plan. Never assume that everything is going to be okay. Never assume that just because a system is in place that it is going to work or that other people's good intentions are enough. You have to assume that at some stage there will be a problem, or that what you expected to happen isn't going to happen. Understand that even if it isn't your problem now, it may well become so later, and at a point where you can no longer retrieve the situation. It is high risk to assume that something will 'turn up' that will resolve the situation.

'Nothing is ever as good or as bad as it seems.'

If your instinct is telling you that there is something amiss, don't ignore that inner voice. There is no point in saying, 'It's not my responsibility' if the outcome is going to impact on you, your project, or the way you function. In an extreme situation, it is a matter of stepping in and saying, 'This is no longer your problem; it is our problem' and taking back control.

Rather than seeing a problem or setback as an obstacle or a difficulty, it can help to look at it as a personal challenge and even something that can be stimulating and enjoyable. There is nothing as satisfying as resolving, to an acceptable outcome, a situation that the majority believe to be insurmountable.

There are times when it becomes necessary to insert yourself or your team into the process of delivery, to make sure that what is promised will be delivered on time, and to be really hard-nosed about it. And that philosophy doesn't just apply to those for whom you have direct responsibility; it extends to external organisations on which you depend to deliver the overall result.

Whether it's getting marketing material printed on time, coordinating ticketing or travel arrangements, or organising security for a major event, it is vital to know that you can rely on your business partners, if necessary by instilling yourself into their meeting structure by having regular progress checks.

The point is that no company, nor we as individuals, can expect others to have the time or inclination to think about our needs when they have so many other priorities to focus on, on a daily basis. Instead, we need to meet with them, explain our needs and ask them to make provision for them. Rather than saying, 'It's not my responsibility to think about how you are going to do your job', or 'What are you going to do about solving my problem?' it is a matter of saying, 'I am working with you because I trust your expertise and I need you to be an effective partner.' Or, 'We need to take an interest in what you are planning because it is our responsibility to deliver an important project that depends upon your service.'

> *'Don't just accept the surface picture.*
> *Drill deeper with appropriate questions.'*

There is a skill involved in never accepting answers at face value and ensuring that questions are asked that diplomatically drill deeper to ensure that the whole picture is known and can be planned for upfront.

ASSUMING RESPONSIBILITY

In every scenario, it is wise to assume that the worst could happen and to make sure that you have a presence where necessary and are absolutely satisfied that future arrangements will suit *your* needs. Rather than assume that business partners are going to take a special interest in what you need to do, you need to communicate to them what your needs are and ensure that all the key players are kept informed of your requirements.

I am not talking about taking control for its own sake. It is of no comfort to the end user if any part of the delivery system goes wrong. Rather than saying, 'Well, we're really sorry, but that aspect wasn't our fault', I'd much rather my own team took a greater level of interest at an early point to make sure we get the right level of service provision, than try to hive it all off to others.

It may increase the workload, it may increase the level of personal accountability, but if we face that early on, it reduces the chance of having to address these problems too late in the process to make a difference when the gaps really impinge upon performance.

The key measures to apply to ensure that a project stays on track are:

- Planning
- Foresight
- Responsibility
- Communication

There is an intellectual rigour required to achieve the best possible outcome in any situation. Again, it is a matter of inspiring business and working partners to feel part of the vision and to encourage them to keep asking themselves 'why' they are involved in the project. In the case of an Olympic Games, yes, it is a project of national importance; yes, it will deliver benefits and services that will be of value to the next generation; and, yes, it is potentially a tremendous commercial venture – but at the centre of it all are the athletes.

If leaders and managers remember that the needs of hundreds of clients and customers are at the centre of all they are doing, they have a template to encourage the right decisions.

CRISIS MANAGEMENT

When an emergency does come at you out of left field, you need to be able to rely upon the quality of your team to make the right judgements, to instinctively understand how to navigate through the situation. It is absolutely crucial. Strategic thinking has its place, but unless you have also got a tactical nose that tells you instinctively what to do when an unexpected situation crops up, you are at a distinct disadvantage.

There have been several moments when crises have hit unexpectedly during my career, most notably when I first heard – on the radio – that I had not been selected for the Olympic team in 1988 (page 183).

Effective communication is important in every area of our lives: business, personal and, perhaps especially, in public life, when living in the spotlight of the media becomes an occupational hazard. The media is so competitive and so 'of the moment' that if there is a story, invariably it will run straightaway. Maintaining the presence of mind to say nothing, rather than succumb to unexpected questions, is often the key to preventing misunderstanding and keeping some personal control of the situation.

That is why any major organisation or high-profile individual needs a good communications team: one that really understands how the media in all its guises works. That means not only thinking strategically about the positioning and profile of a company or team or project, but also being prepared and knowing how to move quickly to avert a crisis. There is only one way to achieve this: *rehearsal, rehearsal, rehearsal* – and ensuring that the whole team understands the importance of the procedure and the need to be prepared.

'Human error tends to be the norm. An effective leader will anticipate problems.'

The lesson is that the best way to avoid major problems in any organisation is to be ready for those problems. Human error tends to be the norm. Mistakes are very rarely down to a failure in technology. Part of the job of any leader is to anticipate crises that might occur in advance of them occurring, and to have in place a protocol and a team of people who know what to do to manage or contain the situation when it occurs.

The risk is, of course, that if you are not careful the whole organisation may develop a bunker mentality, intent upon averting risk rather than focusing on creating a really positive, upbeat project. I think the answer is to ensure that each team remains focused on their own areas of responsibility – so that the creative team does not need to worry unnecessarily about risk management, and the risk management team is respected for what they put in place without being undermined by other departments.

MINIMISING THE VARIABLES

One of the most important things that my coach instilled in me was always to 'minimise the variables'. By which he meant focusing primarily on doing something about the things you know you can do something about. Winston Churchill operated to the same principle. He recommended that you should make two lists: a list of the things you can do something about and a list of the things you can't do anything about. Do something about the things you can do something about – and then go to sleep!

One of the earliest examples of how we applied this to my athletics performance occurred when I was competing as a schoolboy in my first English schools cross-country championships in Luton. In those days, in the 1970s, children would be billeted with host families. It's not a scenario that for obvious reasons happens today.

I remember getting off a coach from Sheffield with the rest of the Yorkshire team, who I didn't really know, and arriving at a draughty community centre before disappearing off with a husband and wife to a suburban area on the edge of Luton with two other team mates. 'Have you had your tea?' they asked. I assumed they meant the cup of tea and a biscuit that I had had at the leisure centre, so I said, 'Yes, thank you' – and that was it. No more food for the day. Racing on an empty stomach was never going to be a great recipe for success. The change of routine combined with lack of food had an impact on my performance, and I finished well down the field.

Later that summer I was billeted above a green-grocer's shop in Crystal Palace. At 4 or 5 a.m. I woke up to hear boxes being unloaded and awnings and stalls being set up. Again, lack of sleep and the disruption of my unfamiliar environment had a negative impact on my performance and I was eliminated in the heats. It only took one more occasion to recognise that the system wasn't working. Very simply, every time I was billeted I lost races.

We decided to go back to doing what we knew *did* work. My coach and I would drive to the event on the day, properly organised, warm up and get to the starting line in good physical and mental shape. It was a system that worked and the results began to improve.

And so you learn to do things in a way that suits you, rather than in the way that may just suit the system or have always been done. But in the early days you need someone like your coach, or your parent, or your manager, depending on the situation, to say with some authority, 'We're going to do this a different way.' I still remember it as a very useful example of identifying and marginalising something that we knew was contributing to failure.

> *'If what you are doing is working,*
> *people will follow your lead.'*

Of course, it's not always comfortable to set yourself apart from the status quo. It is never easy to be the only one that's swimming against the tide. But it is also a kind of training for leadership – to have the courage of your convictions, the courage to be different, to say, 'I'm going to do it my way because the other way doesn't work.' If you do things differently and it delivers results, the lead you take provides a signpost for others.

INCLUSIVE LEADERSHIP

Part of my current leadership role is to remind people that their role, several years ahead of the Games, is as important as the immediate team around the athlete, who are focusing on maintaining their physical and psychological well-being, their coaching and personal support.

I tell people, 'You are such an important part of this

process. You are not some sort of distant hub that doesn't have an impact. It doesn't matter how good the coaching is, it doesn't matter how talented the athlete is. If an athlete underperforms, they get interrupted sleep, or if they miss their event – that's it. The quality of the Games suffers and their years of training are wasted.'

If you can get people to see themselves as part of the immediate team, and to embrace the goals rather than thinking, 'I'm just a contractor, what have I got to do with it?' then the quality of the overall result will improve. If *anyone* doesn't deliver, it doesn't matter how good the show is, it could be enough to derail the project. It is very easy to take time to give the people on your team positive encouragement and this helps everyone to realise that they bring something important to the party.

There is an apocryphal tale concerning President John F. Kennedy that illustrates the point perfectly. While he was visiting the NASA space programme during the space race of the 1960s, Kennedy apparently stopped to ask one of the janitors what his job was. The janitor replied without hesitation, 'Mr President, I'm helping to put a man on the moon.' Those that tell the tale say that the comment is symptomatic of the high morale and clear vision that were typical of the NASA project.

CREATING A WINNING CULTURE

One of the advantages of being a professional athlete is that you are generally surrounded by professionals and experts who believe absolutely in what you are trying to achieve. This is a vitally important aspect of creating a winning culture that works in commercial and public organisations as well. Teams in any walk of life are at their most productive when people are fully engaged in the task in hand and operate as a close-knit team under very clear leadership.

From a leadership position, part of this is ensuring that the work culture is constructive, positive, inclusive and constant.

- It means encouraging open and honest communication
- It means being aware of when to lead and when to allow people to make their own decisions about the most appropriate course of action
- It means making time for people to ask questions. An effective leader will always be prepared to discuss the rationale behind how and why things are being done in a particular way. You can tell a lot about someone from the kinds of questions they ask. Listening to your team is a useful way to identify tomorrow's managers and leaders

- It means allowing people to take calculated risks – within their own area of responsibility – even if it means the risk of failure (provided that failure can be contained). There are times to act and there are times to let things roll. (It's a very instinctive thing)
- It also means paying close attention to the quality of the physical environment within which people work. An effective team needs room to think, breathe, talk and work. These days, remote working and flexible working hours are not only possible, they can enhance productivity too. If managers trust their people, many different work styles are possible
- It means encouraging people to maintain balance in their lives

In a typical week, we often spend more hours with our work colleagues than our families, so the understanding between colleagues and methods of working will evolve and strengthen over time. The level of referral that you expect from a new or inexperienced member of the team is very different to that which you would need from someone who has worked with you for many years. Rather as the coach–athlete relationship evolves over the years, so too the confident manager is working towards creating their own obsolescence, in that you know you are doing a good job if the right decisions are being made even when you are not present.

> *'I now know my job is done, because you did exactly what I would have asked you to do had I been there.'*

As my coach once said to me, 'I now know my job is done, because you did exactly what I would have asked you to do had I been there.' One athlete who became a household name received training schedules every Monday morning in the post. The schedules varied little. On any given Wednesday in the year he knew he would be doing pretty much the same routine. On one particularly snow-laden day it was impossible to complete the scheduled session, as set by the coach. The athlete rang his coach, who told him to use his common sense. 'What do you think he meant?', the athlete asked his training partner, after he had put the phone down. Clearly the athlete in question lacked the confidence to think for himself and take personal responsibility for his own development.

3

THE STARTING GUN

'The heart may pound, but the brain must not.'
Peter Coe, *Winning Running*

Planning, preparation and talent are nothing without the courage to take action. Goals without action have no chance of manifesting as reality; the vision will remain no more than a great idea. In athletics, ninety-five per cent of any outcome may be determined by what takes place away from the track, but the runner's state of mind at the moment the starting gun is fired at the start of a race is vitally important in determining whether or not he or she will be first across the finishing line. In order to maximise the chances of success, there needs to be an element of courage and the groundwork needs to have been done in advance.

A CONSISTENT APPROACH

It may not be a very exciting concept in theory, but races are won, projects are completed and success is achieved only by adopting a consistent approach. This applies not only to the routine aspects of life – a balanced approach to work, sleep, eating and relaxation – but also to planning, budgeting, personal attitude and people management.

As we discovered in the previous chapter, a winning approach is helped considerably by minimising the variables. If you reduce the variables in your situation by behaving in a consistent manner, you are more likely to achieve a reliable and predictable outcome. Think of the laser-like precision of a golfer like Tiger Woods, or the brilliance of Roger Federer, the Swiss tennis champion who has won so many championships with such elegance. They play with consistent excellence. They have rehearsed and practised to such an extent that they minimise the risk of being beaten on the day.

In a business context, it's not just the consistency of the technical advice that is provided or the consistent quality of the production process that is important; it is the constant style of leadership too – ensuring that you have the right people performing the right functions across the team. Your people need to be able to trust your judgement and your approach, and to understand that you believe that they have value as individuals, that their role is important and carries a unique responsibility. It is the ongoing nature of your support and the belief that you have in those around you that affects team loyalty, helps to encourage people to stay with the organisation and makes a difference in the long term.

There may be many people on the team, but on the day the leader is the one in the spotlight and is the one who carries the can.

ENERGY AND FOCUS

The ability to manage time, to remain focused and positive and to block out things that are in a way extraneous to your performance: all these things are crucial to success. The vision and the passion to succeed may drive the focus in the first place, but it is self-discipline, routine and willpower that define that ability so that, under pressure, your nerves can work for you, not against you.

Yes, a race is won and lost in the ability to make the right decisions and bring the right focus to bear at the right moment, but equally important are those decisions made in the three-week build-up to that moment.

I always loved race days and the days immediately running up to them. A race day for me was a day off and was never as physically tough as the average training day. If I had trained properly, I knew that anything I would need to confront in that race would have already been confronted in spades in training. I can honestly say that I never finished any race feeling remotely as tired as I did at the end of most training sessions. In training, on occasions, I ran literally to exhaustion. One of my standard training sessions was six half-mile runs, with a forty-five-second recovery between each one; another was forty 200m repetitions; or sometimes I would run a series of 300m runs, with only seconds separating each one.

Preparation really is everything. It is a principle that I have applied to everything I have done since – and is something that I instilled in my team as well.

> *'Adequate preparation really*
> *is the key to success.'*

Every athlete that you see out there in an Olympic stadium has brought immense focus to bear on that one moment in their career, and that moment has often taken a decade or more to build up to. When they reach that pinnacle, every athlete will have devoted, almost certainly, more than half their young lives to get there.

And, of course, there needs to be balance in all things. Focusing on one thing at the expense of all others will result in a loss of balance. It is possible to over-prepare, or become so absorbed in a task that the overall life-balance is forfeit. Just as an athlete may find it difficult to adjust to 'normal' life once their career has peaked and they are starting to think about other things, so too, in any role, it can be challenging to find a balance between preparation, action and knowing when to stop. So many traits, if taken to extremes, can have a detrimental effect not only on professional performance, but on personal well-being and relation-ships as well.

The same is true in any walk of life. Variety of experience is vital to help the brain and body function and to give them time to absorb information.

But when you are at the start line, you learn to block out everything else. At the immediate moment that the starting gun goes off, the adrenaline is pumping, but there is also a stillness. At those moments, I was barely aware of the crowd. All I was aware of was my own point of focus.

In the build-up to that moment, you need to be able to block out, both mentally and physically, anything that denudes that pool of energy. If you're not managing your emotions, that will take its toll physically.

'You have a finite amount of energy. Your physical and mental energy come from the same source. You're taking both from the same well.'

You have a finite amount of energy. Whether you are using mental energy or physical energy, they both come from the same source. Wherever you are focusing your energy, and however you are giving it form, you are depleting the same well. So to maintain yourself, both physically and mentally, in great shape is really very important. If you are not in control emotionally – in simple terms, you get too nervous, or are unable to control your nerves effectively – then there will be a physical manifestation of that state of mind.

Think back to moments in your life when you were most under stress, mentally or emotionally – you'll notice that you felt tired, and often uncoordinated. There is a physicality about your mental state. Excessive depletion of energy is a contributing factor in stress-related illness and also explains why so many people find it hard to perform to their optimum when their energy is focused on more than one goal. If you can learn how to maintain energy levels, you can also manage and control your energy when it matters.

As an example, through the winter of 1979, before the Moscow Olympics in 1980, there was a lot of talk about UK athletes boycotting the Games. There is no doubt that the uncertainty was unsettling and may have contributed to my disappointing performance in the 800m final (see page 145). I had been preparing since I was twelve for the opportunity to compete. I continued my training regime regardless, on the assumption that I needed to do it to maintain my form, irrespective of whether I went to the Olympics. Had I allowed any hint of doubt to influence me, it would have seriously affected my daily physical and mental commitment. It goes without saying that negative thoughts are not helpful. Questions and feedback can be constructive, but negativity needs to be batted away. That is when the vision that drives the daily effort is so important in crowding out those moments of doubt.

No situation is ever as good or as bad as it seems. Reality almost always sits somewhere in the middle, and life goes on regardless of our individual challenges or misfortunes. The most any of us can do is the best we can do and to keep attuned to anything outside our control that may threaten the overall result.

I am sometimes asked how I manage what some perceive as a high-pressured existence. I have several simple but essential habits that have sustained me over the years:

- To maintain physical fitness. The Latin phrase 'Sit mens sana in corpore sano' broadly translates as 'a healthy mind in a healthy body'. Physical well-being underpins mental vitality and we are better able to manage the challenges and events of daily life
- Enjoying life balance. It is crucial to ensure that no one area of life comes to dominate at the expense of more wide-ranging friendships and interests
- Talking things through with those you respect and trust plays a very important role in effective stress reduction
- Efficient planning and allowing enough time to prepare and achieve things to do them well

PERSONAL ACCOUNTABILITY

From the moment you start guiding others, you are accountable. The starting gun has gone off and the race has begun. Part of adopting a consistent approach in the workplace is about taking responsibility. It's all too easy, when something goes wrong, for people to pull back slightly (even subconsciously) from the project in hand with phrases such as, 'It was nothing to do with me; it wasn't my idea.' I am firmly of the belief that it is important to be accountable – publicly if necessary – so that your team never has any doubt that you are on side, ready to take the rap or to stand in their corner if necessary.

> *'Personal loyalty is a greater driver
> than financial reward alone.'*

There is no doubt that a leader's or a manager's front-line style has a direct impact on the motivation, job satisfaction and performance of their team. Research conducted by The Chartered Institute of Personnel and Development (CIPD) shows that it is relatively rare for people to leave jobs in which they are happy, even when offered higher pay elsewhere. Personal loyalty drives improved performance more effectively than financial reward, on its own, ever could. It is an important point that companies should remember during the current difficult economic times.

My own approach in the face of any crisis or criticism is usually to take the hit straightaway. There is no point in prolonging a negative situation unnecessarily. Confront it, minimise the damage, deal with it and move on – and never show the outside world how you are actually feeling about the loss. It is an approach that is probably familiar to anyone who plays competitive sport and it was never more relevant to my own life than when I missed out on selection for the 1988 Olympics (see page 180). Once you have lost, there is nothing you can do about the result, and there is rarely anyone you can blame but yourself. All you can do is learn from the experience and move on. Remaining stuck in the past of 'if onlys' will merely hamper future progress. Much better to focus on getting it right next time.

There are acute situations, where deals are made or broken, where a similar mentality is required – for example, every day in businesses and households people are working hard to pitch new ideas to those whose money or influence can make them happen, or stop them in their tracks. But sometimes the time is not yet 'right' for decision-makers to feel receptive to a new idea or concept.

On those occasions, it is important for teams to hold together and if necessary to stay true to the original vision and wait until the moment is right – or alternatively create a new marketplace. There is no point in the whole team imploding in disappointment.

It's important, in a leadership position, to keep every situation in perspective and not get too caught up in the ebb and flow of emotion. For example, in spite of facing some obstacles along the way, I knew that it was unlikely that anything would occur during the course of our two-year bid campaign that would be big enough to derail us. Nor was it likely that a single ingenious idea would be enough to push us across the finishing line. In reality those that emerge in pole position over a two-year campaign get more things right than they get wrong. I always knew, instinctively, that if we won the bid it would be, in boxing terms, a points win over the whole distance.

When things *do* go wrong, taking full responsibility may feel painful on occasion, but it is really enlightened self-interest. If your team know that they've got somebody out there who's prepared to step up to the plate to defend them, that means, when push comes to shove, they are also more likely to stand by you or defend somebody else in your team when the situation arises.

TEAM-BUILDING

I have always believed that a good coach needs to know more about the psychology of the person they are coaching than they do about the technicalities of the event they are coaching, just as it is more important for good leaders to understand what motivates the people they are leading than to have a detailed understanding of what they do on a daily basis.

Coaching is both an art and a science, and ideally the coach has those skills in equal measure. But if you were to ask me whether it is the art of coaching or the science of coaching that is more important, I would always say that it has to be the art – because ultimately you are working *with* people. You're working with people that you're challenging to do extraordinary things, commit extraordinary amounts of time and effort, both mental and physical. And although, in essence, the athlete is almost certainly self-driven, the role of the coach is to help them develop in a way that fosters an unquenchable thirst for self-exploration while always helping to navigate the obstacles and road blocks. It is really important that a coach, or a leader, understands the strengths, fears, foibles and weaknesses of the people they work with, as well as what style of motivation they respond to.

'People don't just become excellent; you have to support them, in order to help them to grow.'

If you believe in someone, and they know that, it will feed their self-esteem and bolster their belief in themselves significantly. A winning mind has to be nurtured, and there also has to be consistency in that belief.

Inspiring people is not about flattering them, but about making them realise that you know what they do and understand their challenges and also their perspective. It means developing your emotional intelligence and taking the time to find out why an athlete performs better on some occasions more than others. It means understanding the reasons why a colleague might be a bit sharp on occasion – without taking personal affront. Wherever you go and whatever you do, if you get to know the people you are working with, if you understand their personal motivation, you are more likely to be able to inspire them and to build an effective team.

Back in 2001, I started working in an advisory capacity with a very talented Australian athlete called Tamsyn Lewis. She has won three national championships at 400m, eight at 800m and three Commonwealth Games gold medals. In 2002 Tamsyn had been running remarkably well, but halfway through the Commonwealth Games in Manchester she became unwell after running her semi-final. During the three or four years that followed, Tamsyn suffered a series of injuries and delivered below her potential in three major champion-ships. Of course that was a blow to her confidence, but throughout that period, while trying to deal with injury, she never lost sight of the fact that she wanted to become a world-class athlete. And those of us who worked with Tamsyn over those years shared her belief and saw it as part of our role to help her achieve her goal. It was her coaches' job to help Tamsyn rebuild her confidence and to bolster her self-belief, to help her to return to competitive form.

My coach used to say to journalists, 'Look, this is not a case of "we win, he loses". When he performs badly, I have to take responsibility. This is a really talented athlete, and I am the one who coaches him. When he performs badly, I can't deny my responsibility; I am a part of the process too.' That meant that while he took great pleasure in the gold-medal moments, he also felt not just acute disappointment but also a sense of great responsibility at times when the outcome was not as rosy. Win or lose, coach and athlete, manager and employee, CEO and company – all are in it together. It is a team effort – and it is consistently a team effort. It's important never to lose sight of that.

So it was a great pleasure for me to be sitting just off-stage at the indoor athletics stadium in Valencia in 2008 when Tamsyn won the 800m World Indoor Championships title. It was a great moment, hearing the Australian national anthem played and being able to say to her, 'I told you you'd get there.' Without taking anything away from her success or her brother's day-to-day coaching, I felt a part of it too. And that is the point. Talented people need to be inspired to succeed. Success and failure are always the result of a team effort.

GIVING BACK TO THE TEAM

When you work with a coach, there is a bond. You're in the situation together. If you're training in the foulest of weathers and your coach is at the side of the track, also soaked through, with a stopwatch in hand, you are left in no doubt about the commitment to the cause. In an office environment, the same situation arises. Opportunities to show your support are often more subtle and often verbal, but they are equally important.

When, in July 2008, I had the opportunity to take part in an *Evening Standard* debate about the role of the Olympics and whether it would be good for London, I knew I would enjoy it, but I also wanted to show my team that even in the public eye there are occasions when we must defend our corner. That was my motivation to take part in the debate, because I needed them to know that I believed in them and wanted to defend them.

You can get it wrong, of course. It's not an exact science. But sometimes you've just got to be seen to be out there, alongside and 'on the track', so to speak, to show the world that this is a great team and they are doing what they do very well. Sometimes you need to grab or create the platform to show this.

TRUSTING THE INDIVIDUAL

The relationship between a manager and their team is not unlike the relationship between an athlete and a coach. Over time it becomes a working partnership, with both sides making contributions to the training process and the final outcome. In a successful working relationship it should ideally reach the point where both parties work together so well that each learns to understand how the other thinks and can anticipate concerns and actions.

During my early years of training, from the ages of twelve to sixteen, I would see my coach every day,

sometimes twice a day. He remained my coach throughout my career, but by the time I was twenty he was
pretty comfortable that I would know what I was meant
to do, irrespective of whether I was able to talk to him
or see him before a training session. By the time I was
twenty-five, a whole fortnight, sometimes a month,
would go by without us seeing one another, although
we spoke frequently – often daily – and compared notes.
His view was always that good coaching is about
building in obsolescence: the more you work with
somebody the less you should be needed over time.

Many coaches don't like that concept. They think
that if an athlete starts asking questions about the
training, it implies criticism of what they're doing. In
fact, the opposite is usually the case. Good coaches
realise that once you're getting feedback and questions
you are moving in the right direction. To question is
often a sign of buy-in. Likewise in business, there are
bosses who are so controlling that team members cease
to have the confidence to make any decision themselves. The reality is that most people ask questions
because they are engaged in the process and are
genuinely trying to understand and improve their
performance, to the advantage of the team.

Encouraging an athlete to become involved in their
own coaching can be very beneficial for both parties,

because then the relationship changes. The athlete learns to understand what the coach is looking for and tunes in more effectively to their own physical and mental needs. If after the best part of ten years an athlete still needs to be told on a daily basis what their training regime should be, then the coach has failed to leave enough space for personal growth.

The whole issue of succession planning in business is based upon the same principle of the business leader making him or herself obsolete. Rather than feeling threatened by a younger, talented person, an effective leader or manager will nurture that individual and help them to succeed. A successful company or department should not cease to function simply because a key individual retires, leaves the company, goes on holiday, or takes on a new role; instead, the organisation should already know who the next generation of leaders are likely to be.

Corporate (and training) ethos is most effective if it revolves around performance and function. Just as qualifying times are carefully measured and monitored in order to assess readiness for the next stage of competition in sport, so too, in business, can it be useful to encourage a member of the team to 'act up' to the next level of responsibility – for example, when a senior colleague is on leave, to allow a monitoring period and time for growth and adjustment to the new level of responsibility. It can be a useful tool in selection for future promotion and a talented manager will maintain an awareness of who is hungry and ready for new challenges.

The role of a coach or a manager is not a million miles away from the role of a parent in many ways. Effective coaching or managing is about nurturing and encouraging talent. It's about learning to let go of role and status and helping the people in your care to learn, for their greater long-term benefit. But it is also about taking control and carving out a path if necessary.

In my own case, my father and I got to the stage where he might come and watch a training session and then say, 'Yes, I've seen enough. I wouldn't do anything more or less.' Or perhaps he would offer advice, saying, 'Have you thought about doing this, or adjusting that?' Or, 'Why don't you back off the mileage for a week or two?' His coaching style provided me with useful lessons in leadership that I have often applied since.

CREATING CONFIDENT TEAMS

In many companies there is a tendency to become dependent on an excessive number of meetings. The risk is that they are time-consuming and can hamper progress. I have seen occasions where no one has been able to get any work done, because every time they finished one meeting they were expected to report to the next.

If you give a team permission to go away and do their jobs, without constant sign-off or approval and with full accountability, they will start to develop the confidence to begin making decisions and thinking for themselves. In a highly skilled environment where the right appointments exist, very few people lack the ability to do the job, but a heavily dependent meeting culture will undermine confidence to the point where no one can work without conferring or continually writing reports.

In a work environment where every decision has to be approved by someone higher up the chain, the whole organisation can become paralysed – either because the senior management creates a bottleneck, or from fear that any decision made at a more junior level is a wrong decision. Too much upward referral creates stress for all parties. The junior members of the team end up thinking, 'I had better go and ask,' while the senior members become overloaded and believe, 'I can't leave them to themselves.' It is important to encourage people to trust their own judgement and to allow them to make decisions at an appropriate level.

A senior team that believes in allowing people to take responsibility for their own decisions also allows them to recognise that they can influence the outcome of a project and take ownership of their part in its subsequent success – or failure. It becomes a team achievement.

DECISION-MAKING

Some people are more intuitive than others; they pick up on things that are happening in their surroundings. Anyone in a position of influence needs an element of that skill to ensure that they are properly in tune with the mood of the moment. I know very few Members of Parliament, from any of the parties, who do not have, in their own way, a well attuned social conscience.

When Members of Parliament are in debate across the Chamber, they generally begin from a consensus viewpoint in that they will generally agree on the level of importance of the issue under discussion. Disagreement rarely revolves around core principles of a situation. The differing views usually surround the route to the solution.

Similar differences develop in a business context. In a corporation that has a clear vision, the general priorities will be shared. However, there may well be differences of opinion between different departments as to how those ends should be achieved: the marketing department will have a different perspective from the finance team, whose core considerations will differ from those who are in research and development. But the overall aim of the company is likely to be shared by all involved.

As any athlete will tell you, when you are on the track or in the field you have to make decisions quickly and instinctively, based on a whole range of factors that influence your position in the field. During the adrenaline-filled minutes of a race, the brain operates like a highly tuned computer, taking in every nuance of what is happening around you and interpreting it in a way that leads to fast decisions about how to act based on knowledge and experience. By and large, even though I am no longer competing on the track, I still find that when decisions have to be made very quickly, I draw instinctively on those skills and my first instincts are often right.

There are three key elements involved in effective decision-making:

- Pertinence – whether the decision is appropriate and viewed as the best way forward
- Impact – whether it will be an effective solution and whether it will make a positive difference

- Speed – of the decision, in order to maintain momentum and make an impact

The challenge is to allow sufficient time for discussion and assessment, so that all the key players are involved and have a chance to influence the decision or voice their concerns. Collaboration is important, otherwise there is a risk that the decision will be revisited and chiselled away at after the original meeting, and the original decision undermined.

Having a proper discussion and scoping out the next steps are very important – and the ideal result is consensus decision, though not to the extent that the impact of the original concept is lost. It is important for someone in a leadership role to have the courage of their convictions and to know when to stand firm, accept the risk, or overrule the doubters.

Effective chairing of meetings and proactive follow-through are two of the most important elements of management. It is crucial that everyone feels able to voice their concerns in the meeting – no matter how tough the issues, no matter how personal the concerns – and to achieve 'sign-off' in the meeting forum.

Many people don't like change. They feel nervous about reinterpreting the rule book. My own experience is that just because something has not been done before is no reason not to do it. A new perspective can lead to radical improvement and a reassessment of 'the old ways'. An organisation that is overly cautious or concerned with maintaining the status quo will suffer from stasis and may reduce their chance of winning the day.

4

STAYING THE COURSE

'At various stages in my life people have said to me, "It can't be done." That just makes me try harder.'

Knowledge and commitment on their own do not win races; you need an awareness of those around you, their aims, ambitions and perceptions, and an awareness of the climate of the race. The mid-section of a race has its own momentum and challenges.

The same is true in life, and in business. When the going gets tough, you need to know that others are on board who can keep the vision and pace going. It is about teamwork, communication and maintaining an enthusiasm for that pace, as well as hard graft. You also need to have complete understanding of your competitors – their aims, ambitions and patterns of behaviour.

> *'Failing is part of the process of winning,*
> *and often provides the greatest lessons.'*

The road to gold is not just about winning; it is about gathering experience too. In any field of endeavour, it is self-knowledge and the courage to be completely honest with yourself, and those around you that will provide the keys to future success. I learned along the way that the lessons that we learn from failure are often of greatest value.

NEVER SAY IT CAN'T BE DONE

There have been several key points during my life when I have been told that I couldn't/shouldn't/wouldn't do something, often because it had never been done before. But that is never a good enough reason not to try. In fact, hearing anyone tell me that I can't achieve something generally makes me want to prove the doubters wrong. It is a powerful motivator.

'Couldn't, shouldn't, wouldn't' statements are often based on past evidence or negative assumptions. Just because something hasn't been done historically doesn't mean it is impossible or is a bad idea.

I was told at various points in my career that I would never be fast enough to be an 800m runner and I would never be big enough to be a miler, in comparison to those who had succeeded previously – and yet I broke world records in both distances before my twenty-third birthday.

My coach was vocal in his dismissal of the negative assumptions, and by constructing careful training programmes which developed my strength and stamina, he proved the doubters wrong. I became used to the comments; they simply made me more determined.

I know there have been times when I have fed on the fact that people didn't think I was over reaching. I've actually found that quite a propulsion to succeed. In 1984 all but a handful of people thought the game was up when I missed a gold medal in the 800m; at the outset of our Olympic bid the project was surrounded by doubt at many levels.

There were similar voices of dissent when I first announced my intention to run for Parliament. Many were quick to point out my lack of a conventional political background.

More recently, the decision to send school children instead of dignitaries to Singapore to help reinforce our message that young people were at the heart of the London bid to host the Olympics in 2012 was met with disapproval and concern from many. But a mix of children in our team made a crucial difference in the end.

When everyone believes you are going to fail, you have nothing to lose and everything to gain by proving to yourself that you can do it. Whenever necessary, and with the benefit of experience, I continue to use other's disbelief as a motivating tool when faced with tough challenges.

DON'T ASK FOR AN OPINION UNLESS YOU WANT TO HEAR THE ANSWER

In 1973–4 I lost a full season due to two stress fractures and a whole series of injuries. It was a pretty depressing time. The doctor told me I would never run again. I had been to see a GP who told me that I had an inherent weakness and that I shouldn't really be running at all. With all due respect to general practice, we sought a second opinion. The diagnosis was accurate, but we were unimpressed by the prognosis.

I am instinctively very wary of anyone who ever says

'I'm very sorry but you can't do that', either because it's never been done before or because it's been tried and somebody's failed at it. That's not the same as making a sensible evaluation of where people have gone wrong before and helping them to do things differently, or recognising that failure might have been marginal and could have been dependent on only one or two factors. You have to be very careful about who you ask for advice, because people are very quick to pigeon-hole.

When I was asked to chair the bid, I didn't seek the views of the vast majority of people I knew, because I knew the vast majority of people would advise me not to take it. My gut view was, 'I want to do this. I don't want to hear that there is potential for failure. I already know that!'

The point is, although feedback is important in situations where something has gone wrong, when it comes to making your own decisions about a future action, don't ask someone for their opinion unless you're willing to hear what they have to say.

WINNING THROUGH LOSING

If you look at top people in sport, business or politics, they don't generally just disappear after the first setback. It is not uncommon to find some of the most successful people in business have either been bankrupt, or teetered on the brink of it, or even lost businesses, only to come back even stronger afterwards, having put together things that are actually born of their previous experiences. Rarely is the path to success smooth and accelerated; it just doesn't work like that. But that doesn't mean that the 'failures' don't also have something to offer. Clive Sinclair's 'C5' eco-friendly commuter vehicle, launched in 1985, was widely deemed a failure, but it contributed significantly to progressing research into eco-friendly alternatives to fossil-fuelled transport. He also created many other products – including the revolutionary ZX81 home computer – that are widely regarded as great successes. But they are referred to less frequently in the media. In the USA, conversely, the so-called process of 'failure' is seen as a healthy pathway to gaining experience and long-term success. The American early space missions, many of which encountered problems, each provided vital information that led eventually to the Apollo 11 mission and Neil Armstrong stepping out as the first man on the moon. Failure is not a final result; it is part of the learning process en route to achieving a successful outcome. Failure can, however, be highly damaging if it becomes an attitude of mind.

PRAGUE – 1978

I have won races that have taught me nothing, but I have rarely lost a race that has not taught me something. Competing in my first European Championships in Prague in 1978 provided me with some of the greatest lessons of all.

I was preparing to run in the final of the 800m. It was my first major race against Steve Ovett, and my first time in an outdoor international championship. The media interest that was to dominate our careers throughout the 1980s was already building.

Rivalries in athletics both on the track and in the field have been quite common over the years and in middle-distance running particularly. Our own Roger Bannister and John Landy of Australia chased each other to be the first men under four minutes for the mile; later the UK's Derek Ibbotson ran against Michel Jazy of France; and in 1968 Jim Ryun of the USA competed against Kip [Kipchoge] Keino of Kenya. Keino went head to head with Pekka Vasala of Finland in 1972, as did John Walker of New Zealand with Filbert Bayi of Tanzania at various times during the 70s.

But Ovett and I were different. Not since Arne Andersson and Gunder Hägg of Sweden battled it out for dominance over 1500m and 5000m distances in the 1940s had two athletes from the same country, of similar level of ability, competed against one other at championship level, each of us knowing instinctively that it was unlikely that other overseas athletes would be a serious challenge for that time in our careers. The press sensed the potential rivalry and began stoking the fire.

Just before the 800m final in Prague, I turned to my coach as I left the warm-up track and asked him, 'What do you think I should do today?' He looked at me and said, 'Well, you're not going to win, but if you run as fast and as hard as you can, you'll get on to the rostrum.' And then he added, with a mischievous glint in his eye, 'And we'll find out what the b******s are made of!'

With buckets of adrenaline and his stirring words ringing in my ears, I went off, as the Australians would say 'like free beer'.

I completed the first lap (the halfway stage) faster than anyone had ever done previously in an 800m race.

The tactic worked perfectly, until the beginning of the home straight, when the world began to cave in and the adrenaline was replaced by lactic acid.

At this stage, my focus was not on winning a medal; I was concerned simply with reaching the finishing line! Unsurprisingly, Ovett sensed my plight and smoothly eased past, heading for the finishing line. A matter of a few strides later, Olaf Beyer, the East German, powered first past me and then past Ovett to claim a gold medal and a new European record. Ovett won silver and my doggedness gained me bronze.

'Never doubt that for winners, losing hurts.'

The press gave me an absolute slating that day. I was criticised on every side by everybody – apart from my father, who said, 'That was phenomenal! All you have to do next time is to run the second lap as fast as you did the first!' At the end of that race we both knew that I had much hard work to do if I had any hope of winning in the future. My tactics had raised the form of the other runners as well, so we had also learned a whole lot more about the competition. The outcome of that race was the starting point for reshaping my career in the future. It was probably the single most important defining moment in my entire career. We regrouped to consider the outcome and analysed what we had learnt about the competition, as well as assessing what I needed to focus on in order to win in future.

Just under a year later, in 1979, I applied the lessons learned in Prague to good effect in Oslo. This time I did run the second lap as fast as the first. Adopting the same tactics, but with the physical and mental skills worked on over the previous year to carry out my intention, I broke the first of my two 800m world records. Records which, in total, stood for eighteen years.

Improvement comes from being totally brutal in self-assessment. There was no room for making excuses following my performance in Prague. I knew that if I wanted to beat Ovett, Beyer and others in future, I had to run more miles, improve my strength, refine the track work and increase my conditioning work – and that it had to be done in a more structured way. The same is true in preparing for any role in life.

One more unstructured or haphazard heave would never be enough to enable me to graduate to the next level. The learnings I took from that race provided a signpost for improved performance. They are lessons that I continue to apply:

NEVER UNDERESTIMATE THE COMPETITION

Do your research and never assume that it is only a two-horse race. While you are focusing on challenging your nearest rival or enjoying your position as market leader, others are working equally hard. Never doubt that there is someone else ready to seize the moment and hungry to displace your market dominance. During the Olympic bid, it would have been easy to assume that Paris was the biggest threat to London's challenge, but the other cities were equally hungry for success. We had to differentiate ourselves from the pack.

UNDERSTAND THE PACE OF THE BUSINESS YOU ARE IN

When you are running a race, it is important to know where you are within that race. It's important to keep a clear head. Knowing where your rivals are means that you can adjust your position. On the track this is a very physical response. It means knowing how many paces you are from the person in front or behind. In the marketplace it has more to do with raising profile, enhancing relationships or being aware of others' tactics.

BELIEVE IN YOURSELF

Don't ever make the mistake of thinking that losing is the same as failing, or that losing means terminal derailment. This is rarely, if ever, the case. Winning and losing are one-dimensional judgements that are made easily when you are sitting as a spectator in the stands. Losing once does not mean that you haven't enough talent to succeed in future – it is simply an opportunity to learn, to expand understanding of the task and develop self-knowledge and to find out what improvements have to be made in order to win next time.

FIND OUT HOW THINGS WORK

Go back to first principles. That means asking questions, particularly of those who have shared similar experiences, seeking good advice and making sure that you associate with people who understand what you want to achieve. As a direct result of the Prague race, my father and I chose to broaden our skills base and expand the team of experts whose insight and experience could help me to improve my performance. They stayed with me throughout my athletics career and all remain trusted friends. Even now, because they know me so well, I value their judgements, even when outside their obvious areas of expertise.

FOCUS ON THE TASK IN HAND

When you're under the glare of the spotlight – whether in a sports stadium, the eye of the press or before your peers – while you do need to be aware of the perception of others, you can't afford to obsess about them. Knowing your own ability, pace and position are the crucial factors you *can* control.

GET TO KNOW YOURSELF

Recognise your abilities, appreciate your strengths and work on overcoming your weaknesses.

Losing did not make me want to quit – it just increased my hunger to win. I couldn't wait to get back out on to the track, and I couldn't wait to start making the changes that were needed to improve my chances of winning next time around. But I knew that I should not test myself again until I had mentally and physically addressed and resolved the reasons for failing. As a direct result of my experience in Prague, I improved sufficiently to set three world records the following year: in the 800m (1:42.33) and the one mile (3:48.95) in Oslo, Norway, and the 1500m (3:32.03) in Zürich, Switzerland. Those results would not have happened had I begun training during those winter months simply *hoping* for improvement.

KNOW THE COMPETITION

Understanding your competition is vital in any situation, for two important reasons: it helps you to understand your place in the market, enabling you to evaluate your strengths and weaknesses in comparison, and it also allows you to plan your future strategy and make improvements to better your position. This is not the same as being so preoccupied by the competition that you simply follow their style rather than being at the head of the field. There is a balance to be struck.

It is impossible to lead the pack and to follow your competitors at the same time, but, nevertheless, any project manager, anyone who is launching a new product on to the market, or who is in a competitive situation needs to monitor not only their own strengths, weaknesses and progress, but also those of the competition.

> *'Evaluate your position before you start,*
> *and be prepared to be flexible enough*
> *to adapt to win.'*

There is no point in going into a race without thorough knowledge of other people's strengths and weaknesses. In competitive athletics, the facts often speak for themselves. Before a single foot has stepped on to the track, every athlete will be aware of the win/loss record and performance statistics of those they are racing against. But once the race begins, it is far more physical. You are listening to breathing patterns, tuning in to footfalls, watching the position of shadows and using your brain to judge likely tactics based on previous races and experience. It is now possible to look at the digital screens in the stadium too. If you are on the ball, you will be able to respond quickly when you see an opportunity to open up a lead. An evaluation of the possible shape of the race will have taken place before the race started, but the individual athlete needs to have the awareness and flexibility to make split-second tactical changes while the race is being run. A continuing awareness of the situation from all angles is essential, as is not being so wedded to the plan that you are unable to depart from it.

Assessing the competition in other walks of life can also be quite subtle. In business, it is not unusual for former colleagues to reappear as competitors working for rival companies. Your knowledge of those individuals, their business style and preferred way of working may influence your business strategy in the future. It will give you insight into potential strengths, weaknesses and how they will choose to present their business 'story'.

The reality is that your relationships with your competitors are crucially important.

RESPECT YOUR BUSINESS RELATIONSHIPS

The business relationships and contacts that you make early on in your career don't disappear – they rise alongside you as your peers. People tend to have long memories too, so it is always as well to appreciate your friends and respect your enemies, because you never know who you might be collaborating with at a later date.

Never doubt that in business, as in politics, most relationships are dispensable. Even ones that have been developed over a long period of time can be jeopardised if a contact feels used or misinformed, or if a decision reflects badly on their own position.

That is why it is important always to allow for the space to think about the ramifications and the impact of any action or decision. The more experience we have, the faster and more intuitive those decisions can be made. I found this to be particularly true for me when I moved from sport into politics.

Networking has an important role in every field, but it is the consistency of what we do that is important. Consistency of message, of delivery, of quality. If we are consistent in the way we act and behave in each area of life, then people are able to rely on what we say and share belief in what we do. Few contemporaries in our professional environment know us well on a personal level, so consistency of action is an important tool in securing the relationship.

I'll give you an example of this. As a very young deputy chair of the UK Sports Council, back in the mid-80s I did my first sponsorship deal with Detta O'Cathain, now Baroness O'Cathain. She was Chief Executive of the Milk Marketing Board at the time and she helped secure agreement to sponsor a programme. We called it 'What's Your Sport?' Our paths crossed again later when she was among other roles a board member at British Airways. And now, twenty odd years later, I am asking for her support at a political level to maintain an understanding about the Olympic and Paralympic Games.

That experience twenty years ago means that when I now say I am able to show a historic and continuing commitment to delivering a Games about sport and young people,' she knows that I have not created the idea on a whim. I was knocking on her door even then and explaining why this was an important concept and demonstrating a consistency.

The key is always to inspire others so that they want to share your own vision of what the marketplace might want.

INVITING FEEDBACK

There are times in every organisation when it is useful to understand what people are saying about your work style or leadership ability – and why they are saying it. This was particularly relevant for the newly appointed members of the Conservative team to understand when they joined a party that had been badly hit by losing the General Election in 1997. It can be tough to join an organisation where morale is low and where you are likely to be subjected to criticism for, and expected to defend, events and outcomes that had nothing to do with you personally. In such situations it is useful to listen to the feedback – in order to learn from it – but it is important not to allow it to inhibit innovation or weigh people down.

Honest feedback is important to make sure that you are in touch with the marketplace, but one of the most important things to remember is that the marketplace is made up of people – and every one of those people has the ability to think for themselves. The marketplace could be members of your team or it could be an external market or audience, but, either way, honest feedback is vital to ensure that you are in tune with their needs and that as a manager or leader you are communicating your message and your values effectively.

To receive true feedback, you need to listen first, be ready to take on board negative as well as positive feedback and be flexible in your response. Any team or market or audience is made up of individuals. They are not all the same and their individual needs are different, so they are not all responding to you or hearing you in the same way. You are more likely to inspire people if they know you understand their concerns and you have shown that you are in tune with their needs, hopes and desires.

In politics, feedback is often achieved through focus groups that poll opinions on everything from policies and party leaders to shadow cabinets and a leader's personal image. In environments where people are reticent about speaking up, some sort of managed forum is a useful tool, as it gives people a way to express their opinions. But, actually, my gut instinct, based on working with various teams, is that if you are working in a results-driven environment that environment has to foster an honest exchange and be a place where personal opinions and engagement are respected on an ongoing basis.

Valuable feedback may reinforce or challenge what you are already thinking, and will sometimes reframe your own view and perspective. It is also important to recognise that these insights can and often do come from left field – and not always from the most obvious sources.

> *'Market feedback, from whatever source,*
> *can be absolutely priceless.'*

In the lead-up to the presentation in Singapore for the London bid, I had two conversations with my children that had a profound impact on my awareness of how the marketplace perceived both competitive sport in general and my own discipline of track and field athletics in particular with an obvious read across for other sporting activity.

The first conversation took place in 2003, in Paris. I had been elected to the international governing body of athletics – the IAAF. As a new council member, I took up my immediate responsibilities at the World Athletics Championships that began only a few days after the election. My children joined me (I have four, and they were 5, 8, 9 and 12 at the time). I remember driving down the Champs Elysées from the very nice hotel where we were stopping, en route to the Stade de France to claim our prime site seats; close to the end of the finishing straight, and thinking, as a parent, that I wanted them to savour the moment: and to understand that over the next few days were going to enjoy a pretty privileged existence. I was aware that my carefully chosen words were not falling upon the most receptive ears. The usual distractions of iPods and one son not wanting to wear the seatbelt in the back of the car. Most parents will recognise the scene.

I turned to my daughter, who was twelve at the time, and in an attempt to reinforce the point said, 'Just think, how lucky the children in your class must think you are for being at the World Athletics Championships.'

I'm sure she didn't mean her reply to have the impact it did, but thank goodness she said it. She replied firmly and with clarity, 'Do you know something? I doubt whether there are three children in my whole class who know that these championships are on', or something to that effect.

As someone whose sporting career had been built on the athletics field, it was a fairly searing thing to hear. My daughter was basically telling me that I was out of touch with the marketplace. And she was right. The reality is that the average age of people watching track and field events in the UK is now fifty-six. That tells me that the large audiences that were supporting Steve Ovett, Steve Cram and myself back in the 80s have remained loyal, but we're not connecting enough with the fresh and younger spectators.

Markets change. I am optimistic that the new style of Jamaican track and field athletes who stormed their way to multiple gold-medal victories in the Beijing Olympics in 2008 amongst others will reawaken the interest of the current younger generation. Usain Bolt in particular has the kind of charismatic style that will encourage others to follow his lead. But what was important for me at the time of that conversation was the realisation that my sport was losing ground in the affections of young people and this was food for thought. Given that the excitement and relevance of the Games to that age group was essential for their strength and vibrancy – a movement that could provide a compass and outlet for their values, inspiration and future – and not just be an event attracting an ageing fan base.

Six months later, I was attending a meeting of the founders of the Laureus World Sports Academy, a charity that uses sport as a bridgehead for social change and conflict resolution. As founder members, we have the ability to occasionally invite new members to join the academy. We invite them not only on the basis of an outstanding career, but because they've used sport to engage with people in a much deeper way. Amongst the list of names that appeared in front of me was one that I didn't immediately recognise. It was Tony Hawk, who is the most celebrated skateboarder of all time. I rang my boys at home that night and said in passing, 'Oh, by the way, have you heard of a guy called Tony Hawk?' There was a silence at the end of the phone. My older son said, 'Dad, you bought me his video game at Christmas and I've got his poster on my wall.' And I heard the phone fall to the ground and a bit of a tussle at the other end of the line. My other son came on the phone, saying, 'Dad, Dad, can you get me Tony Hawk's autograph?' And suddenly I realised I was missing something significant here.

In the nicest possible way, the feedback that my children were giving me was, 'You think you're closely connected to this marketplace, and we're telling you you're not as close as you think.' Track and field athletics has been sliding off the radar for my children's generation. What my sons were telling me could not have been clearer. There were other sports more in tune with their lifestyle, competing for their attention. The marketplace was competitive and cluttered and heading in a new and challenging direction for sports administrators.

They were also saying, without realising it, that 'You've got to get to us and excite us. You've got to use technology that is more familiar to us than to you and use it more creatively. You've got to use language we understand. And, even more than that, you've got to excite us about the traditional values that you hold so dear and that you take for granted and place them in a more contemporary setting for us. And you have to do it quite quickly.' We think we communicate with our young people – but, really, in so many ways, we fall short.

The informal feedback that I received from both those conversations, and others, revealed to me the challenge we were facing in the run-up to the bid – and also clarified the narrative that we would take with us.

Every supplier needs to stay aware of the needs of their customers. Price, quality, brand and lifestyle values – there are many factors that dictate whether a product or service is 'in' or 'out' and shame on any leader that does not stay one step ahead of market requirements. There are many examples in industry where the market has been giving the suppliers messages that they have taken too long to hear and adjust to. It is especially relevant in the clothing industry, which has to reinvent itself constantly and where changes in fashion can have an impact on a major brand overnight. In another example, the hi-fi industry that dominated the music market throughout the 1970s and 1980s was gradually wiped out by the new wave of digital technology has largely replaced it. In politics, too, it can prove fatal for a party to ignore public opinion, though it is harder for a political party to reinvent itself or change quickly particularly when in government. In-flight re-fueling is never easy.

Back in 2004, my own challenge was two-fold. I wanted to put children at the centre of the London bid. Sport had played a seminal part in shaping my life and the lives of countless others and I wanted the legacy of the London Games to be seen as being a crucial bi-product of the event itself. The feedback that I was getting was that fewer youngsters spend time in sports centres or arts centres than they did thirty years ago and that trying to engage with young people is becoming tougher each year. I needed my audience in Singapore to recognise and acknowledge that, far from being just a UK problem or a European problem, it is a global challenge – and we need to find an effective solution.

It is a message that every business would do well to understand. Those that are willing to adapt and change will flourish; those that aren't will find it increasingly difficult to survive.

Returning for a moment to the example of Barack Obama, he understood the feedback from his market-place very well, and his campaign made optimum use of new technology. His campaign communicated his message of change via blogs and mobile phones and reached out to young people in a way that no political campaign has ever done before. Of course, the message is only half the battle; delivering the promised outcome is the challenge for every politician. But the point is, he communicated with his voters in a way that they under-stood, and made it easy for them to deliver feedback.

The message that we delivered in Singapore was underpinned by a powerful film that featured children from around the world watching television and being inspired by images of Olympic competitors. Our team did all we could to reinforce the message. We wanted to make it clear that there was no other city in the world that was capable of communicating and engaging with young people in the way that London does. Everything that we have done since has remained focused to that end, and we still listen to the feedback from our marketplace.

KNOW YOUR STAKEHOLDERS

The Athens Games of 2004 was important for us. First and foremost because the British team performed well – but also because it allowed us to introduce Tony Blair, the British Prime Minister of the day, as an important and influential factor in the mix to ensure we optimised our chances of success. Blair has a passion for sport and was a critically important player in the bidding process. His proactive support helped demonstrate to the Olympic marketplace that we were making commitments that had government backing.

It is important in every area of business to have the 'hidden wiring' in place, by which I mean remaining aware that our circles of influence are always broader and taller than the team itself. It is invaluable to have champions in the wider environment who you can count on for support, to have a network of supporters who are familiar enough with what you are trying to achieve to think to send an email or pick up the phone if they think you are missing an opportunity or the competition is in danger of stealing a march. That kind of support gives us the ability to continually understand what the marketplace is saying – and to adapt and react accordingly. When we were planning for the bid, we encouraged that level of feedback on a daily basis.

Support at every level is vital in a corporate or a political context too. Influence doesn't just happen at the point of negotiation – there are other stakeholders that operate further up and down the chain of influence as well. Many of them are invisible. The success of most business proposals is dependent upon getting all of the stakeholders who have an interest in the project to have agreed to it well ahead of the deadline for the decision. Some of these will be internal stakeholders, such as your sales team, production department, finance officer or marketing team, others will be in the broader market-place in the form of retailers, investors, sponsors or suppliers, depending on your field of operation.

The more that individuals within a company can operate like an extended team – not by interfering with one another's roles, but by maintaining an interest in the overall progress of existing projects and new ideas – the more likely that company is to retain the competitive edge.

Even when you seem to have everyone onside, never make any permanent assumptions about people's true opinions. Human nature is such that being successful in addressing the initial concern doesn't necessarily mean you have actually won your customer over. There are probably another three or four concerns to go.

We have a standing joke in our family that sums up this concept well.

We were all sitting round the table one day, while Sunday lunch was being served, and my mother said to my father, 'Peter, how's the meat?' He eventually looked up, probably buried in thoughts about what had been taking place in training an hour earlier, and he said, 'Oh, it's lovely, Angela.' She paused, looked at him accusingly and then asked, 'What's wrong with the potatoes?'

So there it is. There is always the likelihood that immediately after you have answered one question – 'How's the transport plan?' – there will be a short pause and it will be followed by another one: 'Okay, well, what's wrong with the security system?'

In order to have the best chance of winning the bid, it was crucial for us to understand what the core concerns of the IOC might be and where the key points of difference lay between them deciding to vote for London, or for Paris, or any of the other cities. Turning their concerns around and making our answers meaningful and easy to assimilate was probably the biggest differentiator when it came to achieving buy-in to our final presentation in Singapore. The whole process was dependent upon their trust and our understanding of the core issues.

STAND OUT FROM THE CROWD

Differentiation is a crucial aspect of any business proposition. What is it that sets one idea apart from another? Is the idea congruent with the needs of the client, or the customer. When a buyer is faced with a set of similar-looking products, the choice of which one to buy will depend upon whether factors such as value, quality, design or function are the most important differentiators.

That is no mean feat. The project managers involved face the challenge of their lives when it comes to delivering the expected result and the process won't be without its challenges.

'When you have a good story to tell, make sure you tell it properly. Make sure that it differentiates you from the competition.'

Clarity and confidence are important elements in communicating any message, whether it is a bid to win a match, or a bid to win a contract. Don't hide your strengths, because your supporters and your customers need to know they are there. We had to deliver our message clearly. When pitching to become the host city for the Olympic Games, it was important for us that we were not judged as being the same as all the other countries. We needed them to know that we weren't just offering the same old package; ours was significantly different from those of the rest of the pack. And although we were delivering the same types of values, we were offering them in a slightly different way. We started to make that case more strongly too.

The other issue that we needed to focus on was the central message: that the Games provided a once in a generation opportunity to increase the salience of sport in the lives of young people. Many parents will at some point be involved with taking their children to play sport at school, or at a club and those children are the lucky ones. Not all of them have access to sports facilities, and in these days of computers and screen-based activities, getting children interested in active sport is an ongoing challenge. We wanted to show how sport can be used as a bridgehead for tackling so many social issues and problems that we see headlined on a daily basis. Sport can be used to transform the lives of young people in all our communities. That, above all else, was the message we wanted to convey.

TELL YOUR STORY WELL

I knew that I needed to start explaining to people what it was that made us different, how our vision differed not only from other countries' but also from what the UK had put forward in previous bids. Our differentiators were that:

- Sport ran right the way through the project and gave us an opportunity to access other walks of life, other areas of the human condition
- London was uniquely placed, as an outward-facing city with global impact, in a country that really understood the meaning and nature of creativity and diversity and tolerance

It was very important that we also demonstrated that we understood that the Games were moving into a new era. We would not be 'building big' just because the last event was on a large scale; we couldn't put 80,000-seater stadiums in challenged communities without figuring out how they could be adapted for community use once the Games were over. The hard days of the recent downturn have further justified this stance. However, that does not mean a compromise; it means maintaining awareness of the long-term picture. And we also just needed to excite people.

The key to ensuring that the message is read and received effectively is often achieved by working in partnership with the media.

CEMENTING THE MESSAGE

The media are an important stakeholder and it is important to ensure that they are well briefed. If you work with editors or journalists and reporters and understand what their needs are – that their role is to inform and often spark debate and always with deadlines to meet – then there are ways to make the relationship work and meeting differing agendas.

It is important never to assume that the editor of a particular journal will intimately understand the background to the subject and issues or has had a moment to think about how the topic might be relevant to his or her readership. Yet they need to know. They need to understand. And it is part of the role of any business leader to ensure that the message is communicated appropriately. Otherwise editors run the risk of commissioning pieces that are inaccurate and have insufficient inside knowledge to say, 'Hang on a minute, that's not quite right. This isn't how it's been explained to me.'

These days, when I talk about sport, I want people to think about its broader relevance to young people and communities. The more often we talk to people who are in positions of influence and who have strong opinions, the more important it is that we convey that message in a way that can be clearly understood, so they understand exactly what the project is and how it is organised.

When briefing at this level it is important to make sure that you are aware of who you are talking to in advance and who their readership is. I need to do some of their thinking for them. The editor of an arts magazine or the publisher of a niche publication that focuses on railways or farming will have a very different take on the subject from a magazine with a readership that is focused on sport. It is important for the person seeking the coverage to see that there is a news angle that is relevant to them.

It is important to articulate your message in a way that is succinct and easy to understand. During the bid process, in order to communicate our message clearly and in a way that would demonstrate to people that we were different from the other contenders, we commissioned a film to do the talking for us. The directors, Daryl Goodrich and Caroline Rowland, proved to be an able match for Steven Spielberg. Their film showed how the lives of four children from Africa, Mexico, Russia and China are transformed when they watch the Olympics on television and how they are inspired to become athletes themselves. It was reminiscent of my own 'defining moment' some thirty plus years earlier. A picture really does speak louder and more emotionally than a thousand words.

KEEP THE MESSAGE CLEAR

We all like to think that we are independent people who don't care what the world thinks about us. In reality, this is an uncommon quality. My coach was a rare example of someone who genuinely didn't let other people's views influence his own thoughts and actions. I have never known anybody else who was so comfortable speaking his mind. I don't think I ever heard him say anything to me in private that he wouldn't say publicly. He had faith in his own opinions and wasn't afraid of being judged. William Hague is similar. In five years of working for him I never heard him modify anything he said by adding caveats. It's a useful skill to get right – and it's quite brave too. In terms of being a leader, it is a very useful skill to acquire. Clear communication leaves no room for doubt. People understand your message and the direction of your leadership and can respond accordingly.

Of course it helps to be diplomatic and respectful in the way you express your opinions – there is no point in alienating or offending the very people you are counting on to deliver your message – but clarity of expression combined with honesty is an essential communication tool.

5

INCREASING MOMENTUM

'From physical strength comes mental resilience
– and the will to succeed.'

Judging the right moment to change pace during a race, adjust tactics or strike free of the pack takes intelligence, awareness and guts. Everything rides on the decision. Once committed, there is no turning back. The same is true in business. Knowing when to have the courage of your convictions, when to go it alone, when to stick your neck out in the face of considerable opposition – all these are leadership qualities which are needed at the moment when the going is toughest. Energy is not a constant. There are times when there is a need to dig deep and find another gear – while never losing sight of the bigger picture.

ATTITUDE

In order to succeed in any walk of life, and certainly if you want to be a winner in any area of competitive sport, attitude is everything. Not just yours, but the attitude of those around you as well. It's very important to spend time with people who have a very positive outlook on life and who share your vision and the belief that your goals are achievable. Positive imaging and positive feedback are vital to help develop a winning mentality.

That's not the same as having people around you who will tell you, come rain or shine, that everything is perfectly okay. We all need people who are willing to say no to us when necessary and be honest enough to speak up constructively when something needs improvement. It is also vitally important to be able to take that criticism on board and make the adjustments necessary to advance. We each have an important role to play in creating our own luck in life, and it often takes courage to change long-established negative attitudes and entrenched habits of behaviour in order to develop that luck.

NO EXCUSES

It didn't feel like it at the time, but one of the best things that ever happened to me was failing my eleven-plus exam and going to an inner-city secondary modern school. As anyone in the UK who is over the age of forty-five will know, the eleven-plus was a test that assessed which children showed early academic potential. The system was largely phased out in the late 1970s. At the time, there was a great deal of pressure on all children to pass the eleven-plus, because it was synonymous with gaining entry to a grammar school, which was seen as the path to greater academic achievement. However, having failed my eleven-plus, my life took an alternative route, the motivation to succeed on my own terms became all the stronger and I became a more grounded person.

There were two advantages to failing the eleven-plus. The first was that I learnt that failing an exam did not mean that *I* was a failure. The result fed my determination to prove to anyone out there who might doubt it that I had something to offer. If success comes too easily and too early, it can be a disincentive to keep trying. It is the mental equivalent of slowing down as you approach the finishing line. Equally, there is nothing like being labelled a loser from within the school system to make you learn to fight back. There are many present-day leaders of industry who have reacted in the same way.

The second advantage was that it ensured I got to know people from a wide range of backgrounds. The experience gave me more insight than I might otherwise have had of the challenges that some of my friends' families were experiencing during the harsh period of economic recession in the 1970s. This intrinsic awareness of what were the real issues in life became all the more relevant when I entered the political arena.

SEIZE THE DAY

Every profession has its milestones and anyone who is serious about reaching the top of their profession will get there through a combination of hard work, focus, application and sheer talent. However, to be successful in any field it is important to develop an awareness of where you are in the process. If you know where you are in relation to your personal goals, you will understand when to change gear and push on to the next level. Every opportunity has its moment, and if you're not ready for your moment, it could easily pass you by.

The reality is that those who are risk-averse will find

it much tougher, and probably more stressful, to make it to the top in business. At the point at which you make things happen, there is inevitably an element of risk. The tension that is created in bringing all your focus to bear on a single goal will eventually drive you forward to some form of resolution: you will either take the risk and transform yourself by going forward, or take the softer risk-averse option and sidestep the risk of failure but miss out on the reward. The latter is often the safer option, but in the long term it will not enable you to grow or develop as fast. To reach your true potential there has to be an appropriate level of risk management in order to succeed.

One of my defining moments came early on in my career, when I was given an unexpected opportunity to run in the Emsley Carr Mile at Crystal Palace.

THE EMSLEY CARR MILE

In August 1977, when I was twenty, I won the Emsley Carr Mile for the first time (in 3:57.67). Currently a less prestigious race than it was in the past, it has been won by great athletes such as Derek Ibbotson in 1956 (3:59.40) and 1959 (4:03.10); Kip Keino in 1966 (3:53.42); Steve Ovett in 1979 (3:56.58); and more recently by John Walker in 1987 (3:58.75) and Hicham El Guerrouj (Morocco) three times from 2000–02 (best time 3:45.96).

The invitation to run was issued moments after winning an 800m race at Crystal Palace, having just graduated into the senior ranks of the sport. It was a good sign of my progress and growing status in the sport. I was just leaving the stadium when I was approached by one of the selectors. Someone had dropped out of the following day's race due to injury. Would I consider stepping up at short notice? We didn't hesitate. I remember looking at my coach and we both said 'Yes, absolutely'.

The selectors were surprised. They had assumed we would say no, because I'd raced the day before. (In fact, I had also raced *two* days before.) Even having agreed to run, the prevailing advice was not to. 'You ran the day before and you're running against the guy who currently holds the world record: Filbert Bayi of Tanzania.' Others felt that we were setting ourselves up for a very public fall.

We looked at the situation in an entirely different way. It was more of an opportunity than a risk. I had nothing at all to lose and a massive amount to gain, and whether or not I won the race, it would add substantially to my racing experience.

I did win, and I also appeared as a lead story of a newspaper for the first time in my career. It was a race that made the future possible. The so-called risk had put me very firmly in the public eye and ensured that I was one step closer to being selected for my first European Championships.

Making decisions about whether and when to take a calculated risk in life is often largely instinct, under-pinned by knowledge which is in part based on past experiences. You're either ready and prepared to take the challenge or you're not. My first instinct was, 'Yes, I'm good enough to do this and I'm ready for the challenge. I may not win. That's life. I can accept that. But if I'm not there and I don't run, how am I ever going to know?'

It is a story that reinforces the point that every now and then opportunities come your way. If you're not receptive to the opportunity and up for the challenge, you may miss your chance. But you need to be aware enough and poised enough to know when *not* to act as well. Not every opportunity is there to be taken. Each one needs to be considered within the frame of the overall vision or goal.

OVERCOMING OBSTACLES

Napoleon Bonaparte once said, 'Give me only lucky generals.' Actually, I think I would rather have brave generals who create their own luck and who are courageous without being reckless. I am more convinced than ever that to be a successful leader you need to have 'hunters' on your team. By that I mean people with the courage to be trailblazers, with a frontier mentality – like the early pioneers who settled in Massachusetts and overcame a multitude of challenges in alien territory in an effort to forge a new life for their families. Those are the people you need around you when you are trying to win. People who you can trust and who share your vision, people who are committed and are there for the long haul and who will support you whether you win or lose.

> *'Good leaders have a frontier mentality*
> *– they like being pioneers.'*

In 1997, at the age of thirty-six, one such trailblazer was elected to lead the UK's Conservative Party, following the resignation of John Major. His name is William Hague, and he led the Party until he stepped down following the election defeat of 2001. When he initially threw his hat into the leadership ring in 1997, there were plenty of people who immediately declared 'He's too young'. But I remember discussing the issue with William at the time. He looked at me and calmly said, 'The world won't wait for me if I choose to sit this one out. Life doesn't work like that. Doors seldom open again in life – apart from anything else it's the right thing to do.'

You have to be in the race to win it. That's what those with a winning mentality instinctively understand. There are no guarantees in life, but it is rarely worth sitting out the dance in the hope that a more attractive proposition will come along. The reality is that opportunity rarely appears in neatly packaged bundles. The world is competitive and there will always be someone with equal talent, hunger or ambition, willing and eager to take your place.

'Nobody is indispensable.'

William said, at the time he stepped down, 'Nobody is indispensable. Nobody is more important than the Party.' It's an important lesson to learn. We are all dispensable – and opportunities are there to be taken and to be learnt from. Of course, you need to be ready to accept that the flip side of accepting a challenge is the risk that it might not come off. But it's worth bearing in mind that unless your career ends because of reckless decisions it's very unlikely that you will wish you had been more cautious about the way you did things.

William had a vision of what he could bring to the Conservative Party, and he had the courage to grab the opportunity with both hands, in spite of the doubters. It was a brave decision that showed a winning mentality, although few political commentators saw it that way at the time.

The Conservative Party had been in power for eighteen years at the time Hague became leader. The British public, for a plethora of reasons, decided it was clearly time for change from a party that displayed internal divisions. William was initially seen as a unifying element in the Conservative Party. He was tasked with the responsibility of modernising the Party – a brief that David Cameron continues with today – and was responsible for introducing fresh enthusiasm and determination into the teams both locally and nationally. He was an able adversary for Tony Blair at Prime Minister's question time.

The important lesson for me, looking back, is that in reality there probably wasn't very much that William could have said or done that would have made a dramatic difference to his political fortunes at that stage. There is nothing so marginal as a government that slides into opposition having been in power for eighteen years.

William Hague's appointment was made too early in the political cycle to make a difference, but he nevertheless made some valuable changes and was able to advance the careers of several people on his young team. William used to refer to his tenure as 'the night shift'. It's a thankless but essential task – and someone has got to do it.

What the press tries to do at such moments is to capture the mood and give it a label that will last forever. That's their job. And sometimes there's not much you can do about those labels. William was assessed harshly by the press at the time, and many on his team were damned by association – myself included.

However, lives go on and every moment in every life has value in terms of what's going to come next. We all believed in what we were trying to do, and we all shared William's vision. In fact, the majority of the team have all achieved significant success in other roles.

Danny Finkelstein, former advisor to both John Major and William Hague, is now assistant editor and a senior columnist for *The Times*; George Osborne is the shadow chancellor; William is now the shadow foreign secretary and thought by many to be one of the best minds in modern politics. My deputy, Tina Stowell, is now Head of Corporate Affairs at the BBC.

You could say that we each, in our own way, went from zeros to heroes – and we may end up going back there at some stage as well!

The point is that as a team we were able to maintain our own standards, in spite of the fact that the odds were against us succeeding. William was always able to inspire loyalty in his team, and he was unflinchingly committed to the cause. I never once heard him apportion blame. It was leadership you could trust and go the extra mile for.

WHEN THE GOING GETS TOUGH, THE TOUGH KEEP GOING

I was involved with William's office mainly during the general election of 2001 and even the Labour Party will probably tell you that though we lost the election, we won the campaign. Throughout that period we had an obsession with detail, with getting things right. Our campaigns were always well organised and well choreographed. And we did things differently. Traditionally, the Party leader and the senior team in the campaign always followed the press pack during an election. There were usually two main opportunities to meet with or brief the media each day. They needed a news update for the lunchtime slot and something for the evening news and current affairs programmes. We decided that there had to be a more efficient way of utilising the leader's time so that he made local news between the two peak time slots as well. To do this we used helicopters to give us the flexibility to visit any number of locations. We were able not only to brief the national media in the morning, but also to visit several regional television stations or newspapers and many more constituencies that had been achieved in the past.

The benefit of our bullish approach to campaigning, in spite of being at a disadvantage in the polls, is that the structures were put in place now formed the template for future campaigns. Winning is not always about the present. Long-term positioning is important too.

Everything was planned to perfection. Even to the point where we would check the distance that William would have to walk from car to door, to minimise the exposure to unforeseen factors. Walking through open territory is not ideal for a politician at any time, especially during a general election. It doesn't matter how difficult life is – or, in our case, in the midst of the stresses and strains of a general election –

you should never stray from pre-arranged planning unless in extremes.

> *'Always keep to your master plan and*
> *maintain your self-belief.'*

UNDERSTANDING MOTIVATION

A political party's stock-in-trade is trying to motivate people, but one of the risks that political parties run is in not spending enough time talking publicly about things that concern most people. When I became an MP in Cornwall in 1992, once or twice each week I made myself available for people to come and raise any issues that were concerning them. These surgeries usually ran from 5–8 p.m. in the evening. I could count on the fingers of one hand the number of times in a month when I would talk party politics with anybody. Few people come to see their MP, least of all on a Friday night, to talk about the politics of Europe or the situation in the Middle East. They come because they have worries about schools, health, education, vandalism and crime – and usually at a local level. A planning application has been turned down; a parent wants their child to get into a school that is not failing; an elderly woman has had to sell her house in order to move into a nursing home. People want solutions to life's challenges, not to talk about party political ones – although the solutions may well trespass into the party political field.

I recognised most of the issues my constituents were dealing with because, as a teenager living in Sheffield in the 1970s during a time of industrial decline, they were issues my neighbourhood had dealt with too. But I knew they would only be motivated to vote for me if they truly believed that I understood what they were trying to achieve through me as their politician.

That's not to say that you have to have direct personal experience in order to understand the core issues. You don't have to have worked down a coalmine to have an appreciation of the harsh working conditions or how a mine closure might impact on a community, and nor do you have to have experienced homelessness to know its social and economic cost.

There are many similarities, in terms of levels of grit, determination and respect for public opinion, between a successful politician, a winner in an individual sport and an entrepreneur.

COMMITMENT

Most of us confront monumental battles on a day-to-day basis between the brave side of the brain that wants to try for the win and the cautious side of the brain that doesn't want to risk losing. But, by and large, the people who get to the top of their professions adopt a positive 'can do' attitude. They understand instinctively the risks that lie in both approaches. They are committed to achieving their goals and will push themselves as hard as possible to perform to their best, even when the going gets tough.

'There is no certainty of outcome in life, but you will never know what you are made of unless you choose to take part.'

The difference between success and failure, winning and losing, is the acceptance and the recognition that there is no certainty of outcome – unless you put yourself in a position where you cannot compete at all. Winners know that losing hurts. But they're prepared to put themselves into a position of challenge because they know that they will be more frustrated at not having taken up the challenge. A winning attitude develops from a combination of courage, hard work and experience.

MOSCOW OLYMPICS, 1980 – 800m

When you win, it is usually the result of careful planning and a well-rehearsed outcome, or perhaps the result of someone else's error of judgement. When you lose, it is because something happened that was not anticipated, which means you were not as prepared as you could have been. Losing offers scope to do better next time – in every area of life.

A professional sportsperson has plenty of experience of losing and needs to learn how not to allow disappointment to influence future performance. It is a skill that is learned over time. In the 1980 Moscow Olympics, I missed a gold medal in the 800m and won silver, 0.45 of a second behind Steve Ovett. I held the world record for the 800m at the time and, on paper, I was nearly two and a half seconds faster than anyone else in the field. I had been expected to win and so it was a major surprise to many that I came second. I am often asked how I managed to get myself back into the right mental frame of mind to return to the track and take the gold in the 1500m instead, a few days later (the race that Ovett was favoured to win at the time). It is a useful lesson in failure.

It may seem strange to some that a silver medallist could consider second place in an Olympic Games a position of failure, but the reality is that when you have spent the majority of your life planning for and anticipating gold (with some justification), anything less means you have fallen short. Similarly in business, individuals will feel they have failed if they don't reach their personal targets, or if a competitor wins a valued contract. However, you will achieve nothing unless you learn to regroup after a setback.

SHARING GRIEF AS WELL AS GLORY

A good coach will always know how best to respond to the athlete they are working with and what that athlete most needs. It is not unlike being a parent, or an effective manager. If any coach had said to me that day, 'Come on, put it behind you; it'll be okay in a few days' time.' I would have happily dropped them from the nearest window. Falling so badly short of our shared expectations at the biggest moment in my career to that point was a grievous wound. And my coach knew that.

At the time, he was heavily criticised in the media and in private for seeming to beat me up verbally in public after the race. In fact, I understood the real meaning behind what he said and I took no exception to it. When he said to me 'I am ashamed', he actually meant 'I am ashamed for myself as well as for you'. He was telling me 'I don't absolve myself from responsibility for the outcome'. But his words were valuable currency for any journalist at the time. They were not interested in the nuances.

> **'Winning and losing is always a**
> **shared responsibility.'**

His message to me was that a loss, like a win, is always a shared responsibility – in any organisation, or any relationship. When I won, his reaction was 'He wins, we win'. And similarly, as far as he was concerned 'If he loses, we lose'. And he kept asking himself what had *he* got so wrong.

My father had coached me for over ten years. He had created hours of training programmes, had witnessed the sheer physicality of what I had done and had encouraged me as I ran thousands of miles and went through weight-training, commando-type gym sessions and track sessions that were so gruelling I could barely see straight by the end. His contribution to my success to that point had been profound, and he was perplexed. What was it that I hadn't picked up through all that preparation and that he hadn't communicated to me?

But human beings are not machines, and on the morning of that race I felt differently from the way that I normally felt. I was uncoordinated and felt slightly distant from everything. He knew it and I knew it.

As my coach, his dilemma was whether or not to say something to me – and, indeed, what to say. Would he raise unnecessary doubts and risk destabilising me? Should he say something on the assumption that he could discover whatever the malady was and perhaps talk through it? Or would he raise doubts he could not be sure were actually there. It is a dilemma common to every sports coach, every parent and every manager who cares about their people.

My father was a very instinctive person and that is what made him a very good coach. A good coach tends to know more about the people they are working with than they know about the event, which is not to say he was not technically a master of the training arena as well. And, of course, he was my father as well as my coach and I was twenty-two years old – so he knew me well.

Of course, to my mind, it was neither his responsibility nor his fault that when the field started to drift away from me in the back straight I didn't instinctively respond as I had on countless previous occasions. He couldn't be out there on the track with me. Ninety-nine times out of a hundred I would have responded and not allowed that gap to open. In track and field, if you leave that gap to open up, you are dead – and I was.

THE MORNING AFTER THE DAY BEFORE

The night after the disaster of the 800m I slept very well, in spite of the disappointment. Cervantes once wrote, 'Blessings light on him who invented sleep, the cloak that covers all human thoughts.' And it does. Sleep is quite a healer. Before races I used to sleep solidly for a couple of hours. It was an important way for me to switch off my mind, and it is a technique that I still use when under pressure. I used to wake up feeling very refreshed, but with two hours less to mull over the race.

I am sure that many people have had the experience of waking up the morning after a personal disaster and momentarily forgetting the situation they are waking up to. For a few blissful moments I was oblivious to reality, before the pain hit – hard. And I thought 'That was a pretty big loss yesterday'. It *had* to hurt, and I knew it would. If it didn't matter to me, then why on earth had I spent the previous ten or eleven years preparing for that one moment? I felt fragile and almost as if I was standing outside myself and surveying the wreckage of a car accident, knowing only that I had survived.

Painful moments are always hard to deal with. When you affiliate yourself closely with your role, your achievements or your ambition, it is difficult to come to terms with not achieving your objective – whether through redundancy, takeover, missing a personal target or being passed over for promotion.

The key is to realise that you are still in control of your own destiny and to raise your game accordingly. Don't let the failure define you or consume you. Instead, face it head on and take steps to ensure there is no repetition in the future. In my own situation, I had also to remember that there were others who were feeling the pain of the moment too.

William Hague comes to mind in this context. On the eve of his first party conference as leader of the Conservative Party and clearly losing in the polls, *The Sun* newspaper ran a front page image that showed a cartoon of William in the form of a parrot, hanging upside down from his perch. It was deliberately reminiscent of the Monty Python 'dead parrot' sketch. The team were agonising about how to break the news.

When William saw it; he laughed. He could see the funny side. Not only did his humour put the team at ease, he was also able to keep the situation in perspective. Both are highly effective qualities.

IT ALL LOOKS A BIT 'SILVER' TO ME!

The important thing, when you have suffered a major blow or disappointment, is to make sure you have good people around you. We were based in the Olympic Village and, of course, all the athletes shared the same accommodation. My great friend and recently crowned Olympic champion Daley Thompson came charging into my room unannounced. He didn't knock, he just pushed the door straight open, went straight over to the window and pulled open the curtains. I said, rather lamely, 'What's the weather like?' And he replied, 'Oh, it all looks a bit "silver" to me!'

It was the perfect response, and the process of fighting back started. He knew how I must have been feeling, because he is as competitive as I am. He knew I didn't want to hear 'I'm so sorry. You've still got the 1500m'.

In the 800m, it is crucial to stay in contact with the rest of the pack and stay clear of trouble by staying slightly wide of the field. It also gives you a better chance of avoiding the bumping and boring that takes place if you run tightly-packed with the field. Economy of effort derived from an unencumbered race where the margins of winning and losing are sometimes poured over by the jury of appeal in a photo-finish room can be crucial. That's the nature of the race. I had failed to do

151

that and I'd messed up, big time. I couldn't gloss over it. I'd run two and a half seconds slower than usual and I'd made errors of the sort you should be schooling out of an athlete when they are fifteen or sixteen.

There was no point in discussing the situation; there was nothing that anyone could say that would change anything. It was a Sunday. Daley said, 'Just run. Just do what you're good at and go out and run.' There was no point in sitting around. And so for nearly an hour I did exactly that. I just ran. I ran until my mental state had begun to change. It was almost therapeutic. I became so lost in my own thoughts that it took me ages to realise that I was being followed by about ten photographers hanging out of a hire car, hungry for a photo for the newspapers the next day.

The following day was a Monday and I had a very tough training session, much tougher than would normally be undertaken by someone mid-competition. It was more usual to rest at that stage in a campaign. It took another two days, but I eventually started to feel different – more positive about myself and about the coming races.

A NEW ATTITUDE

Before the 1500m final I had to navigate my way through two qualifying rounds. By the time I had finished those, I was beginning to feel different and I was looking forward to the final with excitement, not with fear. I couldn't wait to get out on to the track again. Whereas in the run-up to the 800m I had been thinking, 'Thank goodness I've still got a week and a half to go', this time I was saying, 'I wish I could be there tomorrow. I've got two more days. I'd like to be out there now.'

There was a moment, on the last bend of the semi-final, with less than 150 metres to go, when I made another foolish error. I allowed myself to get caught on the inside of the bend, and I remember at that moment thinking, 'My coach is going to kill me!' Sometimes in those situations you either have to punch your way through or you have the supreme confidence to just allow the rest of the field to drift slightly away and then come round to the front of the pack from the outside.

So as I came round the bend I changed pace and kicked for home. For the first time in that whole period, for the first time that whole season, I felt completely in command, physically and mentally. The pace had changed back to where it had been weeks earlier. I pulled away, up the finishing straight, got the gap, held it. I was back on the stage again.

As I walked off the track, I knew what was coming. My coach greeted me with some well-chosen words from the factory floor. There were a couple of people nearby who had come up through the school of hard knocks, but even they blanched when they heard him. And I deserved every word of it.

THE DAY OF THE FINAL

On the day of the race, I warmed up thinking, 'I feel good, I feel relaxed'. There was no question of my coach being concerned this time. He gave me only one instruction on the day, and that was to stick with Steve Ovett whatever happened.

He said, 'I don't care what happens at the front of that field – you are there. Even if Steve Ovett runs off the track I want you to have left it with him before you even realise what you have done. You'll win this if you are in contact. And if you're not, you won't. It's as simple as that.'

His message was about as simple as it gets.

THE MEDAL MOMENT

There were three of us from the UK in the final: Steve Ovett, a young Steve Cram and myself. At the moment we walked out on to the track, you could hear a pin drop. It was quite extraordinary. There was such an air of expectation. The 100,000 people in the stadium were silent. I heard odd calls, people shouting, 'Come on, Seb', 'Come on, Steve'. But all that changed when the gun went off.

And I prevailed.

After a pedestrian opening – we reached the 800m mark in a time that wouldn't have won the English schools girls final – the race began to pick up.

Jurgen Straub from East Germany had assessed the field and rightly recognised that if the pace remained too slow he would not have enough speed to fight off Ovett and myself on the final straight. With about 650m to go, he picked up the pace violently. This was no steady transition. His aim was to neutralise the finishing kicks of the rest of the field. I knew that I had to follow the pace and Steve settled in behind me. Before long it was clear who the medallists would be. Only the order had yet to be settled.

Straub's pace was relentless. Each 100m travelled a little quicker than the last. It was an effective and clearly thought through strategy. Coming off the crown of the final bend, he was still leading.

Ovett pulled up to my shoulder. David Coleman noted in his BBC commentary that there was unlikely to be any waving to the crowd today. At which point I began my kick for the tape. It took me past Straub, put daylight between me and Ovett, and took me past the finish line.

The lessons learnt from the race are all related to Straub's faultless analysis:

- His bravery led the race and earned him a medal and a place on the podium
- His determination to see the task through meant he was not prepared to allow Ovett and myself to dictate the terms of the race
- Had he just sat in for the ride he would not have won a medal, nor made the race as memorable as it was

They are lessons that are applicable in every area of life.

ELIMINATING THE NEGATIVE

I think that the world separates into two groups of people. There are those who, after a loss, will say 'It's alright, next time it will be okay', without taking the time to figure out what they have to do to change the outcome next time; and then there are those who are prepared to accept the reality of the situation and can see that 'I really need to figure out what went wrong'. The people who take the knocks and take time to understand what they need to do to refine their performance are the ones who eventually bounce back.

Whenever I lost a race, the world looked different. Until I was back on winning form again the feeling of defeat would niggle away at my self-esteem. I disliked the feeling intensely. The way I dealt with the situation is similar to the way I deal with any problem. I review what went wrong and assess what I could have done differently. There is rarely any point in blaming circumstances or other people. As an athlete, I would review my training diary and look at my lifestyle. Were there any tell-tale signs over the previous weeks or months that gave clues to the under-performance?

Sometimes it is necessary just to analyse and accept what happened. I have lost races where there was nothing I could have done any differently; bar not competing in the first place. And that's a perfectly reasonable conclusion to draw on occasions when you know that, 'There's nothing wrong with my mindset, the preparation, the planning – I just got sick or got injured at the wrong time.' There are other times when, if you're honest, you can see clearly that you have simply been beaten by a younger, smarter, fitter or more talented competitor – as was the case when I was beaten in the 800m in Los Angeles in 1984 by Joachim Cruz. You've got to be able to be big enough to accept responsibility and then make adjustments (page 167).

At the end of every competitive season I used to take a month off, partly to have a physical and mental break from training, but it was also my time to take stock in the lead-up to the following year. That month was very important. And at the end of it I just wanted to get back into the race.

'Leaders should be open to change that will enhance their own and their team's performance.'

There is a clear business analogy here. It is vital to develop a habit of conscious reappraisal and to seek feedback when things don't go quite as planned, so that adjustments can be made for the future. Leaders need to remain open to change in order to enhance not only individual performance, but also that of the whole team. It is also necessary to keep yourself 'fit for purpose' – and that includes taking proper breaks and holidays where you have time to recover, review and recharge.

When I look back at my experience in Moscow in the 800m, I think what happened was the result of a combination of a number of things:

INEXPERIENCE

Going to the Olympic Games for the first time is like nothing else an athlete will ever experience – and it can be overwhelming. The reality is that in the 800m final, I was unable to control my nerves. That is why I am so keen that young athletes should have an opportunity to attend a Games without medal pressure. Had I qualified for the previous Games in 1976, I may not have made the mistakes that occurred in Moscow, because I would have had previous experience of being in the Olympic Village, surrounded by other world-class athletes. I would have known what it felt like.

UNCERTAINTY

Until a few months earlier there was uncertainty as to whether the UK team would be going to the Moscow

Olympics. There was much discussion at the time about a boycott of the Games in response to the Russian invasion of Afghanistan. President Jimmy Carter banned US athletes from attending, but in the UK we were given a personal choice.

EXPECTATIONS

The greatest factor in the result of the 800m in Moscow was probably the sheer awareness of the proximity of my greatest competitor: Steve Ovett. He was a prodigiously talented athlete – a talent obvious in his mid-teens. He was usually based over 200 miles south of me in Brighton, but suddenly he was just a few doors along from me in the Olympic Village. I was taking on a guy who looked, to all intents and purposes, to be pretty unbeatable. If I am honest, I was slightly in awe of him at the time.

ISOLATION

In hindsight, I think that I probably spent too much time based in Italy, where I was focused solely on my training. I was in supreme physical shape and arguably the best condition of my career, but I had lost contact with my social and competitive environment.

My surroundings although comfortable were unfamiliar and I became distant from my support team and my friendships. As a result, I probably lost some mental edge.

So the broader lessons in this are that preparation and planning are crucially important, and so is familiarity – with processes, places and people – and connection with others. We all need anchor points to keep us rooted to the day-to-day world we are each a part of which means staying in touch with friends, family and outside interests.

6

THE FINAL LAP

'Life is about marginals at the best of times.
Winning is about timing and belief.'

Winning is a matter of milliseconds, not minutes, days or hours. It is all too easy to slow down once the end is in sight and miss the end target, or to speed up and overlook some of the details in the rush to complete the task. Details matter and maintaining belief will increase chances of success.

A WINNER'S INSTINCT

When you are competing in an athletics competition, or in any sport, there is very little time to think. If you are going to be a winner, you need to learn to make decisions very fast and instinctively. With experience, it is possible to develop a deep knowledge and an intuition that becomes instinctive. The person who is going to bring home the prize doesn't sit agonising over the variables – such as which approach will deliver a forty per cent chance of success and which will give fifty per cent. They have enough experience and have prepared sufficiently well to know instinctively to do the right things at the right time.

It may also be born of an awareness that you really don't want to look back on life in ten years' time and find yourself saying, 'I just wish I'd been braver. I just wish I'd taken that option.'

A winner needs to remain very aware of where they are in relation to their competitors and other factors in their environment. They will recognise when 'now' is the right moment to act, or know how to transform that 'now' *into* the right moment.

ABSORB YOUR ENVIRONMENT

I like to know the physicality of the environment and to become familiar with it. It is all part of the preparation process for the job in hand, because experiences are not one dimensional and we learn and absorb information in a multi-sensory way. By that I mean that we absorb information visually, through sound, smell, touch, feel and also kinaesthetically, in relation to our physical surroundings.

When I was a newly elected MP, I spent hours attending debates in Parliament and getting a sense of the layout of the building and the departments so that I understood how communication channels operated and how everything worked. It was important for me to gain a thorough understanding of the environment – in cricketing terms: 'the line and the length'. It is easier to perform optimally if you are already at ease in your routine and your surroundings.

The role of the Olympic Village is an interesting example of this. It becomes available to athletes in advance of the Olympic Games. Living and training there allows athletes to adjust physically, mentally and physiologically to the social and geographical environment in advance of the Games. In effect, it is a 'holding camp' that becomes a sanctuary and offers a period of adjustment ahead of the main event.

Even though athletes from all nations are competing against one another, they are sharing a unique experience too. As I found when I attended my first Games in 1980, it can be an unforgiving environment to come into unprepared.

In many companies, the role of team 'away days' or training courses offer a similar experience: a time to connect with colleagues, compare notes and tune in to a shared culture and values. Shared experiences and loyalty are powerful tools – especially during challenging times.

As an athlete, I would arrive at some stadiums and just know 'I'm going to run really well here'. For example, I never felt as comfortable running at Crystal Palace as I did in Oslo or Zürich, even though I was running in front of a domestic audience at the South London Stadium. I liked the symmetry and the sense of total enclosure of the Oslo and Zürich stadiums. The geography of Crystal Palace, in contrast, was bitty and there were spaces between the stands. As a runner, I was conscious of symmetry and of running between empty spaces. It was disconcerting, though I never really heard the crowd when I was competing until the race had ended.

Six months prior to the Games in Los Angeles in

1984, I travelled to the stadium and spent time familiar-ising myself with the layout. I wanted to be able to go back into my training and visualise what the stadium looked like. Similarly, I witness some of our potential competitors for the 2012 Games when they visit the Olympic Park, even though the completion dates for venues is still some way off.

LOS ANGELES OLYMPICS, 1984 – 800m

In the 1984 Olympics in Los Angeles I again won a silver medal in the 800m, but in circumstances that were very different from those of Moscow in 1980 (page 145).

I thought I'd be selected for the 800m because I had run comfortably inside the qualifying times earlier in the season, but I was concerned that I might not get selected for the 1500m because I had been beaten in the Olympic trials after having lost almost a year of training due to injury and illness. However, I was eventually selected for both, albeit quite late in the process and in the face of no little media debate, simply put: the press and some of the public didn't feel I was in good enough shape to win.

Whereas in 1980 I was at the top of my game at the

800m distance and my coach and I felt that I shouldn't have lost, in 1984, the circumstances were different. I knew that, for a variety of reasons, I wasn't at peak form for the 800m. And I was beaten on the day by someone who ran better than me – Joachim Cruz of Brazil – and I accepted that.

But winning is not always the only reason for taking part. Often there is a strategic reason too. I wanted to run the 800m not only to compete in the race in its own right, but also as an important step in the process of becoming race-fit to run the 1500m.

> *'Learning to prioritise is an important lesson*
> *in the process of winning.'*

My father was a keen racing cyclist, with in-depth knowledge of the sport. His cycling perspective brought invaluable insight to my training programme. He said, 'Think of this as the Tour de France. The competitors don't start the first stage of the race as fit as they'll be on the last. They develop their physical condition during the course of the race.' Qualifying for and running in the 800m was a way of 'working through the gears'. Competing was part of the process of getting to the 1500m in the best possible shape.

Knowing that I wasn't in peak condition to run the

800m, my coach and I made a very conscious decision. Privately, we prioritised the 1500m as our target gold. Running the 800m maximised my chances of winning the 1500m. It wasn't a strategy that would have garnered much public support had we made our thinking public, but it was a clear lesson in prioritisation and was a strategy that paid off.

LOS ANGELES OLYMPICS, 1984 – 1500m

In a competitive situation, you make instant decisions based on experience. In 1984, when I was defending my 1500m title in the Los Angeles Games, there were three of us from the UK competing for the medals. Steve Cram, reigning World, European and Commonwealth champion, was that day my main rival. For most of the race we followed the leading runners.

I had made the pre-race decision not to allow Steve to control the race over the latter stages. It was a decision born of hard experience and a study of his racing. I knew he was always at his best and most comfortable mentally when he was leading the race. With a long, uninterrupted run for home, I didn't want to allow him to draw upon that strength. And I knew it didn't really matter what happened; I just had to stop him under all circumstances from getting ahead of me in the last lap, even to the point where I knew I was using up one or two gears to keep him behind me at that stage, to keep him from coming past. I had to make that decision at the right moment because he then came up alongside me. In the final push, I took the gold in 3:32.53, which was a new Olympic record for the distance, Cram won silver in 3:33.40 and José Abascal of Spain took bronze in 3:34.30.

But my tactics on the day were born of knowing what made Cram tick as an athlete. There were other athletes who might have come by me at that point who I would have been far less concerned about, as I knew that 15m further along the track I could scoop them up, because they would not have been as comfortable. Steve Cram just loved being at the front of the pack and he was difficult to displace if you let him get there. There were moments in a race when you let him go to the front and he would draw an almost osmotic power from the crowd. He was strong, with great strides, and he loved being ahead with a clear view of the track in front of him. He was never as confident if he was being held off from doing that, and that was his vulnerability. In contrast, I had a very strong kick (I was able to change speed very effectively) and was at my strongest when accelerating off a fast pace. I always prefered to make my move off a slightly faster than a slower pace, even if I had to do something in that race that moved it along, to create that platform.

That's why it frustrates me so much to watch people doing the same old things, even though they have tried the same tactics previously without success.

Time and again, athletes put themselves into a position where they can't possibly win a race. They are given opportunities, but they don't take them. In sporting terms, if you have run the same way for the last fifteen races and have finished outside the top places each time. There is little or no chance that scenario will alter unless addressed.

Whether in sport, in business, or even as a parent, there is no point in doing something the same way and hoping that somehow the outcome will change this time – because it won't. The outcome is predictable.

Dame Kelly Holmes, in contrast, is an example of someone who adapted her tactics to tap into her strengths and it paid dividends on the greatest stage.

DAME KELLY HOLMES

In the Sydney Olympics in 2000, Kelly Holmes won a bronze medal in the 800m. It was a medal against the odds and it was a medal she won only because she was brave enough to get herself into a winning position.

Four years earlier, I was sitting with her in a London restaurant, and she said to me, 'One more injury and I'm out of this sport.' In spite of taking a silver medal in the 1998 Commonwealth Games, she had been battling with illness and injury for the best part of five years. Mercifully, she didn't get another major injury. She made it to Sydney and she scrapped her way to that medal. Kelly took the race on in the finishing straight, and put herself in a position to grab a place on the winners podium. Although she was overtaken by two other athletes in the final few metres, a bronze medal was a fantastic achievement given her recent history of injuries. She had to be very, very brave to get that medal.

Kelly was thirty that year, and I suspect she thought, in her quieter moments her chance of gold had slipped by. After all she would be well into her thirties by the time the opportunity came around again. I was in Birmingham with Daley Thompson when I watched her qualify for the Athens Games. Her 800m was so comfortable and commanding, and she was clearly approaching a purple patch of form. I turned to Daley after she ran that 800m and I said, 'If she does that in Athens, she will win both the 800m and the 1500m.'

Kelly worked through another set of difficulties and

injuries over the next four years, but she did qualify for the Athens Olympics – and she did win both races and became only the third woman in Olympic history to achieve the double.

But for me, it was equally impressive that Kelly ran so commandingly over the four qualifying races. She ran absolutely foot-perfect throughout. I was deeply impressed by Kelly's apparent ability to break down winning gold into bite-sized chunks over the qualifying heats.

Presenting Kelly with her medals in Athens was a moment of immense personal pride for me – but not before I had helped her undo her track shoes and encouraged her to warm down after the race. She was so overwhelmed she had forgotten to take off her spikes. Although she spoke at the time about being an emotional wreck after winning the first gold, she still managed to steady her mind and maintain her focus well enough to come back to do it all over again later the same week. She no longer had anything to prove to herself or anyone else, but she maintained her focus and her hunger and won the double and a place in the record books.

Kelly has shown true winning mentality through the good and the bad times during her career. She is an outstandingly brave athlete.

MENTAL PREPARATION

The philosophy that I maintained during my training years I still apply to my other major commitments in life.

- Remember that ninety-five per cent of the preparation takes place before the event
- Make sure your team is prepared
- Stay true to your game plan – but retain the flexibility to react to the unexpected
- Do what you need to do to stay relaxed

In the hours before the final presentations to the IOC in Singapore in 2005 I chose to go for a run and I went shopping for gifts for my children, rather than joining the anxious throng who were gathered around the TV sets outside the main hall. My colleagues asked me, 'Don't you want to watch the other cities' presentations?' When I said 'No', I had to explain, 'There is nothing more I can do. All these cities are competing for the Games. You know they're going to be good. What can we do if they've thought of something that we haven't thought of? Nothing. We can't suddenly put it in to our presentation. It doesn't work like that. There's nothing any of us can do at this point.'

You can't suddenly walk out on to the training track, having watched somebody else in a heat, and think, 'I'm going to have to do three more training sessions.' It can't be done. The work has to have happened ahead of time.

For me, it was more important to prepare mentally for the speech I had to make later that day. I knew delivering the speech required absolute focus, and anything else would have diverted my attention.

I also knew the team was fully prepared. The last thing anyone needed was me sitting there telling them what they already knew they had to do. We had finished our final rehearsal the day before. Everybody knew that if any one of us gave anything less than an Oscar-winning performance, we would not win. And on the day, everybody played their part superbly. I planned my time to get down there at the last possible moment and walked straight into the hall.

WORD PERFECT

I do a lot of public speaking. My own style of preparation is write the initial piece in full, and then to revisit the material. Gradually, over several revisions, I whittle it back to the key trigger words for my speech. It is a method that I have evolved over time, because I don't like reading coldly from a speech, though I will have the paragraphs and structure in my head.

There are other occasions where an unexpected news factor comes into play out of left field and the carefully crafted speech goes out of the window. And then you roll with it. You either use the news piece to your advantage, or you say, very assertively, I'm not here to talk about that, I'm here to talk about this – in best political fashion.

When I gave my personal speech in Singapore as part of the team presentation for London 2012, I wanted to use my own words. I felt passionately about what I wanted to say, and the team had been rehearsing the message for a long time. I had been playing around with the content in my head for the best part of a year and a half, testing phrases on different audiences, testing lines that I wanted to use. The speech was well rehearsed in my mind and had been through various previous forms – but suddenly, at 4 o'clock in the morning by a poolside in Singapore, and feeling very jet-lagged, I felt ready to put on paper exactly what I wanted to say. I wrote the words out longhand.

We knew the speech had to be very precise. Every word had to mean something. My template was really simple: if I said *anything* that day, that anybody else could have said there was no point in me saying it. If the Mayor of Paris, or the Chief Executive of the Madrid bid, or Moscow or New York could say it, then that didn't put us ahead of the game. I was the only one that had an Olympic competitor's experience. I had to make that count, and I had to make it different.

TAKING A BREAK

I don't like meetings that run into each other without air and space. If you're not careful, as you go from one meeting straight into another, you remain mentally where you were twenty minutes ago. So if I can manage it I will arrange for a short break between meetings and I'll walk quite a lot during a day.

Time is always at a premium in business. My diary tends to be managed by other people and when your whole day is spent with other people, bliss is having a day to myself with nothing to do and with no commitments.

'Even the busiest leader must know when to switch off and recharge their batteries.'

On rarer days I will take time out to go to an art gallery, listen to some jazz or get on my bike and spend time riding or running around London. I may break for a bit, have a cup of tea and continue for another couple of hours. You just have to do that every now and again: do something completely different. It's really important. I don't take the mobile phone with me. I literally switch off.

I know I'm lucky, because if anything was a real problem, someone would probably know how to get to me. But my philosophy is also that if you are in a senior management position, and you have done your job well, then there are other people on the team who have the knowledge and experience to make an appropriate decision. And if it's something that only you can deal with, then probably on balance it's going to be alright until tomorrow anyway.

The brain needs periods of rest in order to allow new information to bed down, and fresh ideas and perspectives to come to the surface. There are numerous accounts through history of people making new discoveries when they were relaxing or taking a break from the very thing they had been focusing on; Newton and Einstein are two extraordinary people that come to mind.

It is much harder to give form and focus to new ideas at the same time as receiving a constant stream of new information. And yet we are living in an era where the majority of people are unable to be separated from their mobile phones for the length of a car journey. If we are not careful there are no periods of calm, and we become at the constant call of others' demands. There is a constant need to be in contact with everyone the whole time – while, ironically, we seem to be losing the art of conversation. Text messages and emails are a very different form of communication. It can take children, in particular, a very long time to switch from Web-based activities to ordinary conversation. Likewise, in athletics, performance will often be enhanced by a period of relaxation and calm after taking short periods out from formal training. On the same principle, athletes returning to competition after a period of injury will often perform much better than expected.

Exercise in general is critically important for anyone wanting to perform to their optimum in life as in business. When I first joined William Hague's team as Chief of Staff we discussed the importance of getting in shape for the job in hand. William worked extremely long hours and had to travel extensively. A politician's lifestyle is both physically and mentally taxing. He wanted advice on how best to increase his strength and stamina and opted for judo as a means of getting fit. Under the guidance of Ray Stevens, (Olympic silver medallist in Barcelona in 1992) he qualified as a blue belt very quickly. All too often when under pressure of time, exercise is seen as the less important priority. My own view is that physical health feeds mental agility and is a vital aspect of being an effective leader.

STAYING CALM IN ADVERSITY

Not everything in life turns out as planned. Sometimes sheer bad luck or an unexpected event can create a momentary crisis that will take you off course and force you to reassess your vision and future priorities.

That was the case for me when I failed to be selected for the 1988 Olympic Games in Seoul.

I was nearly thirty-two years old at the time of the Olympics in 1988. Throughout 1987 I had been dogged by an Achilles tendon injury and so had done relatively little competitive racing in comparison to previous years. I went into training that winter with the renewed excitement that only an Olympic Games can generate. Championships were for me what racing was all about. But of all the championships, the Olympic Games is the one that galvanises the excitement of everyone.

Over the course of a career in any profession, different skills present themselves at different stages.

During my first Olympics in 1980, at the age of twenty-three, I was physically in great condition but mentally too inexperienced to cope comfortably in the pressure cooker of an Olympic year. During 1984, I had a different set of challenges because I had been ill the previous year, but by the time of the Games I was mentally much more resilient than I was in 1980. I'd had four more years in the sport and the benefit of those experiences. So by 1988, with my third Games in sight – even though I was older than many of the field – I also had more self-knowledge and more confidence than I did in 1984. I was on form and confident that I had every chance of being selected.

In 1980 and 1984, the Games had taken place in August. The 1988 Games were scheduled to take place in Seoul, South Korea, so the dates were scheduled for later in the autumn instead, to provide more benign climatic conditions. Clearly we needed to modify my training regime in order not to peak too early. There was a risk involved in taking that approach because, traditionally, British Athletics teams are selected only weeks before the Games, in June and July. That year the dates of selection remained largely unchanged even though the Games were later than usual. We knew I would enter the selection process slightly 'undercooked'.

Midway through my training programme, in June of

1988, I was told by the British selectors that I needed to produce a qualifying time in the 1500m to partly satisfy some of the selection criteria. To break my training routine when we still had many weeks left to meet the full criteria was a concern and inconvenient, but, nevertheless, at short notice and with some help, we were able to set up a small town race in Switzerland, where, virtually on my own, I ran the requisite time.

Mission accomplished, I returned hours later to the training camp. Unfortunately, I also picked up a cold around that time. And from that point on I was struggling.

Almost immediately, I had to return to the UK to run the British trials, where I finished fifth in the first heat. That was no marginal loss. I wasn't posing selectors a delicate problem on the basis of having narrowly missed out on the first two places in the final. I came fifth, and I was struggling to breathe.

Ninety-nine per cent of the population, had they felt as I did that day, would have gone to work as usual, feeling below par. As I would now. I just happened to be in an occupation where a cold is a very big problem. Anyone who has tried exercising with one will know that it takes its toll. To be even one per cent off form in world-class athletics makes a dramatic difference. Rule number one – 'Don't run with a cold'. In hindsight, I shouldn't have competed. But I knew that if I didn't run in the trials, I wouldn't be selected. It was a *fait accomplis*.

The drive back to Loughborough with training partners that evening was made in silence.

At that point, I was considered a safe bet for selection to run the 800m. I had run the fastest time that year in the UK. But I knew that my berth in the 1500m was at risk.

On Sunday, the chairman of the selectors rang me up to ask how I was. I explained that I had a cold and it was agreed that as long as I could show that I was fit and healthy in the next two or three weeks, that I would make the team.

'Perfect,' I said. I would see the team doctor and get myself sorted out as quickly as possible. I then planned to go to one of the big track meets, like Zürich, and run the qualifying time.

The next day I drove to Guildford to meet the team doctor and was advised to take a few days off before resuming training. On the return journey I tuned into the 3 o'clock news, only to hear the blunt news headline that 'Sebastian Coe's Olympic career is over.'

The General Athletics Council had met that morning. They had voted thirteen to twelve not to select me for the Games at all, in spite of the reassurances from the selectors the night before. They had been overruled.

By the time I arrived home, there were reporters standing three deep outside my front door. At least I knew why they were there. I needed to control my emotions and I would have to think on my feet. I didn't want to say anything I would later regret. Later that afternoon, I issued a statement to the press, making two comments. Firstly, I expressed my disappointment at not having been selected; and secondly, I made it clear that I was looking forward to resuming my athletics career later the same year. I wanted to say, as clearly and calmly as possible, that, 'You may not want me to compete in the British team anymore, but it's for me to decide when to retire.' I explained that it had become clear that I would not be wearing a British vest again and that this was a great personal disappointment, but that I wanted to wish the very best of luck, fitness and form to those selected.

The phone rang constantly over the next few days and I was offered any number of possible solutions: Indian citizenship as a result of my mother's family background; Belize offered me a passport. Of most significance was the offer of a wild-card entry from Juan Antonio Samaranch, president of the International Olympic Committee, which was a tremendous act of faith but which opened a political and diplomatic can of worms, and was later forced to retract his offer. There was even a campaign run by the *Daily Mirror* called 'Coe Must Go' – the same paper that campaigned against my inclusion in the 1984 team!

There were many things happening at that stage that were not purely to do with my athletic performance. In every area of life there is a hinterland that may not be focused entirely on whether you are the best product in the marketplace, or whether you have made the most compelling case for something. In my case, whether I was the best athlete for the task ahead. There were any number of reasons why those on the committee felt I should not be selected – not least because there was a sense that the next generation of runners should be given an opportunity to show their form. That was an argument that I had to respect and which I accepted.

In the meantime, I just kept my counsel and planned to go on holiday. In that way, I regained control of the situation.

But, of course, it left an enormous void and no little irritation and disappointment. I was in no mood to sit out the Games watching my events on television. I walked into a travel agent one street away and booked a ticket. While the races were being run in Seoul, I was on a small island off the coast of Italy.

MAINTAINING DIGNITY

It was little consolation that the winning time in the 1500m at Seoul was the slowest for many years in an Olympic final. The lesson, however, is to know yourself well enough not to be affected or deterred by others' decisions.

The lessons I learned from this, and which have been invaluable to me, are several-fold:

- I don't like reacting to a situation publicly until I know the full facts. Because an off-the-cuff, emotional response is really only of value to journalists. When they ask a question, you need to instinctively ask yourself, 'What is it that they really want, and why?'

- Focusing on my own disappointment would have served no one. An Olympic team member represents their country as well as themselves as an individual. I understood that pressure and didn't want to add to it. To say that I felt I had a better claim over other people would have placed an unacceptable burden on a team who were already on a tough path

- It was a time for others to make judgements. It was not for me to demand that I should go. There are some moments when you are best served by maintaining a period of radio silence

- Don't allow important relationships to fracture. Clearly, I had allowed relationships to break down to the point where a general council felt little difficulty in making this decision. Sometimes that means taking the lead in fence-building and standing back from the fray enough to be objective

Had any of my team turned around at that time and said to me, 'Actually, they are right, you shouldn't have gone', or 'You know, you're not worthy of a place in that team', I would have taken that very seriously. But they were not saying that – in fact, far from it. What they did say was 'I don't think you should remotely consider calling it a day', and the training log and physiological assessments suggested I was still performing as well as I had been three or four years previously – which shows the value of maintaining records and always monitoring performance, training and competition.

I knew that there was an identifiable reason for why I had underperformed. It wasn't that I had lost the ability to train hard, or bring mental commitment to the task in hand. Those things were just as strong as ever. I had had an injury the year before, but most athletes get injuries from time to time. It was simply down to a heavy cold and a dose of very bad luck.

FIGHTING BACK

There was an enormous void and I was undeniably disappointed, but I was not ready to retire. I decided that I could now pick the points in the season that I wanted to aim at free from championship racing and selection trials. I didn't have to worry about selection trials for anything.

I knew I needed to get back into an uninterrupted competitive season – and I returned to the winter months with renewed focus. Though for the first time in my professional athletics career, I entered the 1988–9 winter training season without any expectation of being called to compete for my country. It wasn't a big selection season because it was a post-Games year. I just focused entirely on running in races that I enjoyed going to. I spent time on the Italian circuit early in the season and started running well.

By the end of the season, in 1989, I finished top of the ranking list at 800m, 1000m, 1500m and 1 mile in the UK, was placed second in the world at 800m, and gained a silver medal in the World Cup in Barcelona at the end of the season. So, at the age of thirty-three, I had one of my best seasons. I had also been recalled to the British team.

> *'Sometimes you have to believe in yourself*
> *enough to create your own marketplace.'*

You have to create your own marketplace sometimes. When a door closes in one area, you have to go out and create your own opportunities.

The reality is that selectors have a very difficult job to do. Whether in sport or a group of investors making a key financial decision, selectors make a judgement based on what they see at the time. And they don't always get it right.

There is a fiendish delight that comes from reading about a successful venture that has been turned down by seasoned investors only to hear that a year later the owner has won a £4 million contract and the business is now burgeoning. It is the stuff of *Dragons' Den*, but it happens in real life too.

In times of adversity it is important to maintain self-belief, personal esteem, and to practice the principles that have served you well.

Don't fold up. Don't keel over. Don't just say, 'I take your word for it.' Ask questions, reassess and then decide whether your product is good enough to keep fighting for. You should certainly take the advice of experts and sometimes do things differently.

Balanced against that, if you intrinsically know there is little wrong with what you are doing, it is more a case of fine-tuning than of radical change.

SUPPORTING OTHERS

When things go wrong, there is a tendency for others to want to speak up in defence of the wronged party. One of the challenges facing my close team when I wasn't selected in 1988 was agreeing that we would all maintain a silence. Second- or third-party endorsement is nice, but it's not that meaningful when it comes from within the organisation. Rather than doing you a favour, other people's well-meant words can often make things worse. The team got together and agreed that we needed to put the events behind us, have some fun and prove everyone wrong. I think my coach was caught off-guard at one point and had a few choice words to say, but, by and large, we controlled the situation very well. Sometimes you just need to squeeze the oxygen out of a difficult situation with a period of determined silence.

There are times when you need to meet things head on, but it tends to be when you are defending others, rather than when the situation relates to a personal goal or vision.

If you do need to explain a situation, settle very carefully on the message and the messenger. Some months later, I chose to put on record my interpretation of the saga in an interview with the respected television interviewer Brian Walden. I felt that was the most appropriate mechanism for a considered response, and so much better than an off-the-cuff, knee-jerk reaction.

7

BRINGING HOME
THE FLAME

'If we win, I will carry the flame home;
if we lose, I will carry the can.'

Every great achievement in life, whether in business, politics, education or sport, is the result of thousands of smaller and very important steps taken in preparation. Every area of life has a rhythm and a pace. The moments of success are important and they are hard-won, but they are neither the beginning nor the end of the personal journey. They are important symbolic milestones that can be shared with others and provide the motivation to strive for further success.

FOR THE JOY OF RUNNING

Throughout my career, I relished the toughness of the training regime, because I knew that the more I pushed myself, the closer I was to becoming the best in the game. Without that passion to succeed, the end goal would not have mattered, and I would have chosen to do something else. But it wasn't until towards the end of my athletics career that I realised quite how much the love of the physicality of running was my true motivation.

I can remember the day that I decided that I would retire from competitive athletics as vividly as if it were yesterday. At about 6.30 a.m. one crisp and beautiful October morning in 1989, I was running along the towpath of the River Thames, from Richmond to Twickenham on the outskirts of London. I was two miles from home and the sun was starting to break through the layer of mist that sat above the river. As usual, I was thinking about all kinds of things as I ran, including what I could do to improve on the past season during the forthcoming winter training period.

At every point throughout my athletics career I had been able to visualise areas where I could improve my performance and what I needed to do to achieve that improvement, whether by making changes to my conditioning programme or varying the terrain or climate that I trained in or the balance of training loads. Year on year I had been able to recognise what I needed to do to improve. At that moment, it suddenly dawned on me, and with some certainty, that there was nothing more I could do to run quicker. I had reached the peak of my ability and now it was time to stop. It was a defining moment – not a sad moment or a tragic one, but a moment of realisation. The gut feeling was very strong and very clear, and I have since learned never to ignore that inner voice once I have heard it and the sentiment has been thought through carefully.

> *'My true motivation stemmed from the sheer, unadulterated joy of running.'*

Had I been asked ten or fifteen years previously what motivated me to keep running, my answer, inevitably, would have been the desire for the prize – to win a gold medal and ideally a world or Olympic record. Now, as I ran along that towpath, I realised, with great clarity, that my motivation stemmed from something much more than that. It was the sheer, unadulterated joy of running, of meeting the challenge of turning myself, sometimes against the odds, into a world-class middle-distance runner – the best I could be. Winning was of course important to me, but had I not truly loved what I was doing, the medals alone would not have been enough to keep me motivated or to fire the imagination.

The self-motivation, determination and discipline that I applied to the track are applicable when striving for further successful outcomes and overcoming obstacles in all areas of life and at every management level. Competing is exciting and winning is exhilarating, but the true prize will always be the self-knowledge and understanding that you have gained along the way.

People often ask me what drives me and whether I set goals for myself. The reality is that I knew what I wanted to do from the age of fourteen. I have always had a strong sense of where I am headed and where I am in terms of achieving that overall picture. However, I rarely set immediate goals that would take focus away from the primary task in hand because it is impossible to give one hundred per cent attention to two tasks at the same time. So I did not begin to actively take steps to begin a career in politics until I had already started to think about retirement from sport. Now that I am involved in the process leading up to the 2012 Olympics, I don't get distracted by thinking about what I might do next as I am focused on achieving my current goal. Every project is four or five years in the making, and as the end of each period approaches I begin to develop a plan for the next four or five years.

I also tend to only take on projects and challenges that excite me. That is very important for personal motivation. That means if I am faced with an aspect of a task that is repetitive or laborious, I can appreciate if not always enjoy it for the necessary part it is playing in taking me towards reaching the overall goal.

I am inspired by the coaching team and the commitment and expertise of those around me. I enjoy working with a team of people who are at the top of their game. There were key moments in my career when a significant number of people dedicated a great deal of time and effort, often in a voluntary capacity, to help me to achieve my goals. Without wanting to sound too trite or clichéd I do feel that I have a genuine responsibility to try to do as much as I can to deliver similar opportunities to the next generation.

The outcome of any competition is the result of hard work, natural talent and great coaching, mentoring or training. If any one of those is missing, there will always be a limitation. But luck can also play its part. Most of us can look back at key moments in our careers and think, 'Well that success was really marginal. It could have gone either way', or, 'That failure was as much down to a stroke of bad luck as it was down to a lack of something on my part.'

In every field, success or failure tends to be defined by pivotal moments: winning a medal, losing an election, winning a sponsorship deal or losing a contract. The large periods of time spent working and preparing in between those moments that shapes the ultimate result. All you can do is to manage the aspects that are within your control and have the flexibility to make use of a stroke of good fortune when it comes your way. The gods do need to smile on us occasionally to help make things happen.

A MATTER OF PRINCIPLE

Great coaches and strong leaders not only impart great skill and great knowledge, they also help to create an ethical framework and an environment that encourages excellence. If an organisation shares an ethos that is strongly enough entrenched in the behaviour of senior management and heads of teams, those shared attitudes will permeate throughout the organisation. When positive behaviours and attitudes are shared by parents, management or peers it becomes counter-culture to behave in a way that is contrary to that ethos. But, of course, the reverse is also true. Negative environments will also have a profound influence, never more so than in areas of social disadvantage.

The question of drug abuse in sport is for me a profound one. It is important because I could never have compromised myself in that way, and nor could the vast majority of my fellow competitors. I am either good enough at my craft or I am not. I have either trained hard enough or I haven't. I either possess the talent and the skills or I don't. If I don't, it's not a crime; that's competition. But pretending you're something you're not is a different matter. If I am not good enough, I have two choices: either to work harder and smarter and differently, or to choose to do something else instead. It really is very simple. Never knowing whether you would have been good enough to win without chemical enhancement would have been unbearable.

'Not being good enough is acceptable. That's life. But not being good enough and pretending you're something you're not is not acceptable.'

Drug abuse in sport – as in any other field – undermines the whole achievement. Winning depends on the quality of your preparation and training, the way you think through schedules, knowing the right days to work hard and the right days not to and the excitement of working with a team that has a shared goal that they are trying to help you to achieve.

But cheating in any capacity, in any field, is an insult to you, those you are working with and the rest of the field – and ultimately it destroys self-knowledge and self-esteem.

There is an argument that drug use is related to the modern commercial pressures to perform well. I am not a great believer in that argument. Performance-enhancing drugs were in evidence long before the advent of modern sport and the era of commercialism. There is well-documented evidence of athletes in the ancient Games, as long ago as 55BC, experimenting with dried figs and other potions. In the late 1800s, strychnine was being used to improve psychological and physiological endurance.

All pressure is self-induced. If something isn't working, the answer is to take stock and ask some hard and soul-searching questions before adjusting future behaviour. Masking the problem with drugs or a web of excuses will simply make the pressures worse next time.

'All pressure is self-induced.'

It's an important issue not only in the context of setting a leadership example in the broadest sense, but also because if we are to remain true to our message that London 2012 is about young people, then it is vitally important that our anti-drugs message is out there and that we have in place adequate measures to try to ensure that there is no question of illegal drug use by the athletes who are competing or by anyone connected with the Games in any capacity.

Self-regulation is an important aspect of any team and any company. Staying true to yourself and taking care to maintain a set of shared principles within the team is very important.

STAYING ALERT TO A CHANGING MARKET

Markets and competitors are constantly evolving and changing, perhaps never more quickly than in the fields of sport and politics where careers can be made or broken in a matter of moments. During the time of my Olympic career there were some radical developments in racing strategy that had a profound effect on my own training programme.

Although I was acutely aware of Steve Ovett as formidable competition from an early age, I think it is fair to say that he was not too bothered by me until our paths crossed seriously in 1978. I was a year younger than him, with some way to go. By 1975, when I got to the European Junior Championships, Steve was already a seasoned international, having won the European junior title for 800m in 1973, followed by a silver in the senior event in 1974. In 1976 he went to Montreal with good chances at both the 800m and 1500m. I narrowly missed out on competing at Montreal that year.

It was a big year for me. I remember watching the Games on television and seeing not just Ovett, but also Alberto Juantorena from Cuba, who won the 400m and the 800m running so powerfully the athletics world shook. He led the race from the front, taking everybody with him, with strength and no little style. He simply ran them off their feet.

A similar thing had occurred when, in 1974, I sat with my coach watching Filbert Bayi run the whole 1500m from the front of the pack in the Common-wealth Games, creating a world record and beating a very strong field. I remember my coach saying, 'Middle-distance running is never going to be the same again.'

When, within two years, Juantorena had done pretty much the same thing. The world had spectacularly moved on. The training manuals and operational manuals had been rewritten. Throughout this period of change, I was reassured by the approach we were adopt-ing. At that moment, it supported our own decision to focus our attention on speed-endurance, enabling us to optimize the distribution of effort with the requisite physiological underpinning.

More recently, Usain Bolt has had a similar impact again challenging some conventional thinking in the sport. The most extraordinary thing about Usain Bolt is that, at his height of 6'5", most coaches would instantly classify him as a 400m runner. The assumption being that any athlete with legs as long as Bolt would be unlikely to pass through the sprinting phases with a cadence quick enough to challenge at the distance. And that would be error number one. Because Usain Bolt is different from the last person who walked through that door at 6'5". It is unwise to make snap judgements on surface appearances. There is no template because everyone is different. A 6'5" athlete has now become the 100m world record holder.

If anyone had asked me at the time whether the Ovett effect had any impact on the way I was training, I would have absolutely, resolutely said 'No', because my coach was determined that what we were doing was the right way to do it for me, regardless of the quality of the competition. But there is absolutely no doubt that there were moments in the training cycle when he did influence my attitude to training.

Of course, there's nothing like having a sharp

competitor out there to help you raise your game, but, at that point, if I'm being honest, I thought of him as being an obstacle to my progress. I wasn't sure in my own mind how I was going to navigate the situation, because, on paper, he was quicker and stronger in pretty much every event.

But, again, this is where the leadership role comes in, and a consistent approach matters. My father refused to alter our game plan. Steve ran very much more mileage than I did and as my coach his response was, 'Fine, that's perfectly legitimate. That's how *he* comes to competition. That's not what works for you.'

In 1977 Steve Ovett ran one of the best 1500m races of all time, by winning the World Cup in Düsseldorf late in the year, so by the time our paths crossed again in the 800m during the European Championships in 1978, I was more than aware of him as a formidable opponent. I lost that race (see page 99), though it was critically important in my development.

Then, in 1979, during a year when Steve had eased up on his competitive programme in the lead-up to the Olympic Games in 1980, I broke three world records in forty-one days, literally only weeks after graduating. He probably then began to realise that I was quite a serious threat. I sensed at that point that it had stung. And for the first time, on paper and on the ranking list, he was no longer number one.

Later, in the winter of 1979, during the lead-up to the Games in Moscow, I remember training on Christmas Day. It was a harsh winter (harsh enough to bring down a government, amongst other things) and I'd only recently returned from Rome. I ran ten to twelve miles on Christmas morning, before Christmas lunch. It was a hard session and I remember getting home, showering and feeling pretty happy with what I had done.

Later that afternoon, sitting back after Christmas lunch, I began to feel uneasy, but not quite sure why. Suddenly it dawned on me. I thought, 'I bet he's out there doing his second training session of the day.' I put my kit back on I faced the snow and ice and did a second training session. I ran several miles, including some hill work.

Not long ago, over supper in Melbourne, I told him the story. He laughed. 'Did you only go out twice that day?' he asked.

But the key lesson for me in all of this, looking back, is never to change your game plan because of something that someone else has done. Your needs are different to your competitors' and if something needs to be changed, it should be done in a careful and conscious fashion: strategically and over time, not in reaction to someone else's aims. Strategy relates to long-term goals, whereas tactics are the practical manoeuvres that need to take place on the day. Short-termism should never replace the long-term view.

ONE STEP AT A TIME

It is crucial to remember that nothing of substance or long-lasting quality will happen overnight. Nothing sustainable happens quickly. You have to be dedicated to the goal and you have to be patient during the gestation period.

It took me ten years from the outset of regular training before I entered an Olympic stadium for the first time.

'Nothing sustainable happens quickly.'

If you were to ask any successful athlete or sportsperson the secret of their success, most of them would store much credit in their coach. Good coaches know that they are not going to create a world-beater overnight; they know that it will take years to help shape a winner from raw talent. They also know that there will be periods of time when progress plateaus or occasionally slows, where nothing seems to be changing or happening. But each step is an invaluable building block.

Likewise, if you were to ask the majority of business leaders whether they made it to the top on their own, most would acknowledge the influence of others at a critical point in their progress.

The top people in every field also know that the hours are long, the work is hard – almost remorselessly – and they probably have to come to terms with the personal sacrifices involved fairly early on in their careers.

BACK TO LIFE AS USUAL

Adjusting to life after a career as a full-time athlete is very difficult. When everything has been geared for years to achieving a single goal, there is often a personal chasm or void when the career is over. The decision to change direction or leave a profession is a very personal and often difficult one. But it is even more profound when it's a way of life where physical frailty or age demands that you simply can't continue with doing something you are passionate about.

Immediately after the 800m at the Moscow Olympics I thought, 'I don't want to do this anymore.' And yet, when I came into the finishing straight during the lap of honour after the 1500m, I can remember already planning ahead to Los Angeles four years down the road. Having completed my mission, I could allow myself to start thinking about my next goal. And when I came out the right side in Los Angeles, I remember going to the beach with some friends and talking to them about it.

'Should I go on? I'm twenty-seven – this is a pretty good moment to leave. In many respects, there's probably not a better moment to leave, now that I've done what no one has done – won them sequentially, back-to-back.'

And I remember my coach was quite clear that it was my decision. He would have been remarkably sanguine if I had decided that was enough then. But, actually, I decided that I genuinely enjoyed what I did and that I would keep going for the next four years. At the next Games I would be thirty-one. That meant four more years of hard training and wear and tear, with no guarantee that I would make the Games. I made a conscious decision that from this point onwards, that medals and records were a bonus. I had to start putting other things into place.

I knew I wanted to be involved in politics and when I was invited to join the UK Sports Council I recognised it would be a useful experience for life outside the stadium. In 1984 the then Sports Minister asked me to chair the Olympic Review Group, which was to meet the concerns of governing bodies of sport that did not have enough resources to properly prepare elite competitors for the Olympic Winter and Summer Games in 1998. Little did I realise at that moment that this would not include me (see pages 180–185).

I agreed to do it, as I felt it was important, but only on the condition that there was guaranteed government money to deliver the promised results at the end of the process. The Sports Minister agreed. I also made it clear that I wanted to choose my own people to involve in the project, and not necessarily those who were steeped in sport or from traditional sports.

A CHANGE OF GEAR

A few months later, three hours before running the Golden Mile, I sat with John Rodda on the balcony of the hotel, agreeing drafts of the report. I would never have allowed that degree of split focus even a year earlier.

I had rationalised that I'd won two Golden Miles and I'd broken the world record. Although this was a really serious race, it was also really important that I get this done. John was also a member of the Sports Council committee and was covering the Golden Mile event for *The Guardian*. So, I suppose, in my own mind, I had begun to make a few compromises. I raced three hours later and I lost the race, and my world record, to Steve Cram.

That's when I knew that I'd changed a gear. Although I wanted maintain my primary focus on athletics, I also had to develop a hinterland for myself.

I became Vice Chairman of the Sports Council in 1986 and I remained in that role for three years until 1989, when I became a parliamentary candidate.

ENTERING A NEW ARENA

When I entered politics, I knew that I was choosing a profession where few others would come from a sports background. I was embarking on a career where those with years more professional experience in politics were likely to question my expertise and my motives, where political instinct would not be seen as compensation for lack of experience, whatever that experience might be.

The questions were predictable. 'Why would you want to become a Member of Parliament?' was a recurring theme. What in essence they were questioning was why I would want to depart from the comfort zone of an activity that I was noted for and certainly familiar with, in exchange for one I was not. There were of course other things I could have done. My keenness to go into politics, although never articulated throughout my athletic career, was a driving force within me.

Most people come into politics and gain a much higher social profile. Conversely, I went into politics and got a much lower one.

The point here is that the only person who can understand your driving passions is you. If you are willing to take the risk that something may not work out in order to pursue a heartfelt ambition, then don't let anything stand in your way. The important thing is to understand why you are making your choices and to maintain a clear understanding of your overall strategy.

I knew that I would enter politics, even before I became involved with the Sports Council. And I hoped that the role would give me greater understanding of government and the public sector – which it did. So by the time I was twenty-nine, I'd written two reports for government – one on Olympic funding and one on drug abuse in sport – and I'd discussed with Secretaries of State and Home Office ministers how we could enshrine in criminal law the carrying and trading of anabolic steroids in sport. It gave me an insight into the machinery of government.

I instinctively understood, within quite a short period of time, that politics is the arena of scarce resources. The best cases win; the badly presented get nothing. I also understood that what we weren't doing very well in sport was making very strong arguments. So we were missing out.

I voiced my concerns to Richard Tracey, the Minister for Sport at the time, and we commissioned a report from the Henley Research Centre about the economic impact of sport. I sat down with the Trades Union movement and the CBI determined to show that this was a very serious sector of the economy. The forty-something million pounds a year that sport received was derisory compared to the contribution made to the overall economy. At that point the sports sector was the third or fourth largest single employer in the country behind the car industry, coal and petro-chemicals (how times have changed). More sports goods were being sold in the high street than records, tapes or whatever was current at the time. It was a £3 billion sector of the economy.

The political interaction was a fascinating process and I soon understood was that there are buttons to press in order to get things done and buttons to leave well alone. I then began to think that doing this on behalf of constituents would be an interesting challenge.

MP FOR FALMOUTH AND CAMBORNE

I applied for a constituency in West Cornwall, rather than opting to contest a safer seat that I could have won with a more comfortable majority. The competitor in me had resurfaced. I did not want anybody to think I had been parachuted in for an easy ride.

Timing in life is everything – so they say. Becoming an MP in a party that had held office for thirteen years was never going to be a comfortable position. Cornwall was going through a transitional phase. The fishing industry was contracting, adding economic challenge to an already hard-pressed area, and the last tin mine was about to close. Looking back we were probably always destined to leave office after one more term.

People say to me, 'When did you know you were going to lose your seat?' And I tell them, 'About fifty seconds after I won.' My agent showed me the percentage of the vote. It was 36.8 per cent of a three-way split. And I thought, even then, there's no way I can hold on to this seat. I was sure I would be voted out in five years' time. So, in a funny sort of way, it gave me an independence of thought while I was there. I thought to myself that I would do it my way.

BODY LANGUAGE

Sportspeople are very good at reading body language. When you watch the way people warm up in a race, you notice how confident they are, how relaxed they are, how they handle themselves and what they say before a race. You learn to know whether they are just going through the motions or whether there is an excitement – a hunger in their eyes or whether they would rather be anywhere than facing a competition.

When I was on the political campaign trail in the 1997 election, I probably picked up the mood of the electorate quite quickly. Many of my colleagues were saying 'they're being really nice to us on the doorstep. We thought this was going to be so much harder than in 1992.' I was seduced by this attitude for a couple of days, until I realised, after speaking to one woman, that, 'No, you're not engaging here. For a very good reason you've made up your mind and you want me off your doorstep.'

In 1992 the electorate was angry, but they were still

engaged. This time around they were almost benign, not looking me in the eye. No one wanted to say, 'I don't want to vote for you.' The quickest way to get rid of us was to be nice. They didn't want to argue anymore. They'd just run out of interest.

There were two important realisations for me at that point:

- You know you're engaging with politics when someone is actually giving you a very good run for your money
- The one thing you cannot ever allow yourself to do in politics is to take failure personally

I knew that, like most of my colleagues on either side of the House, I'd worked hard to be a good MP. But there are some things that you can't control. Sometimes you are just in the wrong place at the wrong time.

It was an interesting experience for me in another way too, because when I raced in a British vest, most people (apart from Steve Ovett supporters) wanted me to succeed. Within three years of leaving professional athletics, I was in a profession where, at that point, a larger part of the population didn't want me to succeed and I was being viewed in a very different way – with suspicion. Suddenly I was a political being.

TRANSITION PERIODS

Once an important period in your life comes to an end, a period of transition begins, as you shed your old view of yourself and add a new layer of interest and experience.

In many ways, transitions are easier in commercial life than in sport, because the whole model of progression is based on the assumption that you will be promoted over time, move jobs, perhaps even move to another country. There may be a period of adjustment as you leave one working environment and enter another, but, broadly speaking, unless redundancy or a radical change of direction comes into play, there is a consistency of purpose.

In contrast, transition periods for top competitors can present a real challenge. In order to reach the highest level in sport, or even in politics, there has to be a real passion and commitment to the cause. Any professional sportsperson knows that the moments of glory are transitory. The bigger reality is the challenging routine of training on a daily basis. Success means preparing and rehearsing by doing work that borders sometimes on the repetitious. As an athlete, I developed an appreciation of the repetitive nature of the training and an awareness of the importance of the detail. You soon understand that it isn't going to happen unless you are willing to do that. And you need to be ready to keep doing that when you change direction or move up in your career.

When you have been wholly involved in creating something, to the exclusion of almost everything else in your life, it can be very hard to find something else to turn your attention to that demands the same level of single-minded focus. In the case of an athlete or someone in the public eye, it can also be a challenge to do without the support network that tends to offer protection from the mundane nature of managing everyday life. The impact of a sudden change in pace, focus and lifestyle can put a great deal of pressure on the individual and on family relationships. The ability to cope with this style of transition is less to do with leadership and more to do with self-awareness. It is a lesson in life-balance in the broadest sense.

The reality is that those who focus on one aspect of life to the exclusion of all others are bound to find the transition more difficult than those who have had an alternative profession from the outset. It can be hard to realise that although you have spent much of your life being told you have an extraordinary talent, it's not always a transferable talent.

When, a week after finishing my last race in Europe,

in a World Championship in Barcelona, I was one of thirty-six other candidates, hoping to progress to the next round of interviews for a constituency in Falmouth and Camborne. It was an extraordinary juxtaposition. Extraordinary, but it's what I wanted to do. I was confident enough to think that I'd make a good MP, but I also recognised this was leaning heavily on skills originally grasped earlier in an entirely different activity.

I learned that although my talent was not a transferable skill, the training process and mental application definitely was. It was a different kind of pavement-pounding this time.

Just as an entrepreneur who builds up and sells a successful business is often simultaneously regrouping and starting something new, so too someone who is changing profession focuses on a new idea underpinned by all their previous experiences. Although coming in at basement level, your previous experience and the knowledge gained generally means that you will progress more speedily than if you were learning from scratch first time around.

TIMING IS EVERYTHING

As an athlete, the point at which you decide to change gear and focus on the next stage is very important. I always get slightly nervous when I sit with anybody that says they don't know whether to go on for another four years or not, because it generally means they are thinking, 'What else is there to do?'

For those who are planning to earn their living talking about, writing about, or even coaching their sport, timing may be less of an issue. It becomes more and more important, the older you are, to become aware of where you are on the pathway of your career and when to choose to change your position.

SUCCESSION PLANNING

As people progress in their careers, ambition often takes a new form. Many senior managers and directors take great satisfaction from becoming a conduit for the next generation of achievers. The winning mentality becomes less about them personally and more about passing on knowledge and experience to others.

> *'Good leadership includes looking towards*
> *a future in which you pass on your*
> *responsibilities to others.'*

As part of my chairmanship of London 2012 I've got a group of really talented people leading our teams. It should be a built-in responsibility of organisations to make sure that whatever the workforce does, they are better placed and skilled to do it when they choose to move on than when they joined. Not to feel threatened, but actually to recognise we have the bottom line to think about, the delivery of whatever it is we are hoping to deliver, but also the development of people within the organisation – both spiritually and physically.

Of course, it's a more complicated process now. At the time of the bid we had a team of 60 people. Often we knew each others' families. We're now up to 300 people and by the time of the Games we will have 3,000. It's not possible to know everyone by name. That's why it is important to have carefully structured management teams, so that development will take place within those teams. With dozens of new people joining every month, you can't get to know them all, but you can make sure that there is a framework or an environment through which they can flourish and you can tune into their ambitions, fears and challenges.

Epilogue
THE TIME IS NOW

*'The answer to life? You get out what you
are prepared to put in.'*

As I look back on my career so far, I get a huge sense of satisfaction from all the high points – those moments when hard work, self-belief, determination and sheer bloody-mindedness have seen me through and met the objective – whether that is crossing a finishing line in pole position, or standing up and fighting for something I believe in.

But I have equally drawn strength and insight from the moments that did not go my way. I hope that throughout this book I have conveyed that nothing of significance or lasting merit comes without some kind of investment; be it time, energy, belief or enthusiasm. All are vital components in achieving success. You certainly don't get excellence on the cheap.

Bearing this in mind casts the moments of setback and failure in an all-together new and different light. I can't say I ever enjoyed losing at anything – few people do – but what I can say is it was in those moments of doubt and uncertainty about the next step that I really learned something about myself and about the nature of my resolve to emerge stronger and better placed to tackle the challenge. Although it didn't feel like it at the time, finishing second in the 800m at the 1980 Moscow Games and losing my parliamentary seat in the 1997 General Election were as important in my development as a person as the more obvious highs.

> *'There is nothing quite as rewarding*
> *as proving life wrong.'*

When faced with any setback, it is natural to look for an easy way out or even blame circumstances or individuals. In an ideal world, someone else would simply pick you up, dust you down, pat you on the back and invite you to 'go again'. But if we genuinely want to succeed, a period of re-assessment and affirmation of our original vision and goals, together with a healthy dose of grit and determination goes a long way. There is nothing quite as rewarding as proving life wrong.

Of course it's not always possible to find the necessary well of strength solely within ourselves. In these times, the answer lies is drawing on support from someone whom we respect and trust. Throughout my life, my source of inspiration has more often than not been my coach and father, Peter. He was a truly remarkable man. I am eternally grateful for all the times he pushed me and inspired me to dig deeper and be the best I could be, even if sometimes there was room for improvement in his media-handling skills.

I have also drawn tremendous strength from my wider circle of family, friends and colleagues who form an invaluable support network for me. Having children, as any parent knows, is simultaneously exhilarating, exhausting, frustrating and at times challenging. The responsibility for helping shape and steer the dreams and aspirations of young people should sit heavily on our shoulders. Perhaps that is also the essence of my motivation and commitment to the Olympic and Paralympics Games; not just 2012, but the metaphor for life that the Games represents for all of us. If life is a series of moments, both public and private, the

Olympic Games represent the ultimate realisation of an instance when sheer hard work and determination are rewarded and true spirit is celebrated.

Sport has been an ever present part of my life. Success, stimulation and the enjoyment that is derived from active participation in sport is analogous to how to get the best out of life. I have seen time and again how sport acts as the hidden social worker in a community. The litmus test in any country is how we embrace excellence. The volunteers in local sports clubs are often unsung heroes who freely give their time – literally hundreds of hours of every year – doing things for young people and connecting with them in a way that many official bodies never achieve. Sport helps young people to develop self-esteem and personal skills at a vital and formative time in their lives.

The same is often true in a business context too. Informal mentoring, apprenticeships, coaching and ongoing training – all these things are immensely important, not only in engendering confidence and commercial awareness, but also in building and maintaining a sustainable corporate culture. Leaders, managers and coaches in all professions need to ask themselves at each stage of a task and on a daily basis: How can I help the next generation to learn and grow? How can I encourage my team to prepare well and consistently, but also learn from their mistakes? How can we pass our experience on to the next generation, and how can we encourage them to share their ideas? The business world is going through a period of tumultuous change, but I firmly believe our compass is to focus on these core values.

LOOKING FORWARD

Looking back is also a prelude to looking forward. While I feel incredibly privileged to have got to where I am on my journey through life, I also have a set of goals that will drive me on in the future. Some of those goals are currently in the forefront of my mind, and will demand my attention now, while others are yet to be fully-formed or articulated. I have always benefited from having clear, well-defined goals.

I do not profess to have mastered success by any means. Success is not a product, it's a process. I am in no doubt that adopting and applying a winning mind is key to that process and unlocking its secrets. Success is not some kind of exclusive club where you can simply pay your membership dues, sit back and let life's rewards come to you. The nature of success is entirely determined by the individual. Success for some – quite legitimately – is getting up in the morning. For others, it is about changing a perception, overcoming a fear, rising to a challenge or sticking to a belief. Success can be either large or small, noisy or quiet, light or profound. Success is whatever you want it to be. Although some start life with natural advantages or disadvantages, there is always an opportunity to rise above a given set of circumstances, and make the world notice you. I look forward to the day when as few of us as possible accept the status quo and instead push for something which cannot be grasped without effort. Modern life has many distractions and there is a rapidly developing culture of instant gratification and worship of the cult of celebrity. But human existence has always ultimately been about the search for meaning, and nothing is quite as meaningful as achievement that is hard fought, precious and lasting in its impact. Such thoughts were certainly powerful motivators for me in the daily grind of training or when picking myself up after a setback.

Whatever your field of endeavour – whether you are a budding sportsperson or an aspiring executive or business leader, my advice is to understand and absorb the lessons life throws at you, to focus on your goals, to continually challenge yourself and never be deterred by seemingly insurmountable opposition or odds. Once you've decided what you want to achieve, commit yourself fully. There are no half-measures. Then and only then will you find out what you are really made of. You may just be surprised by the results.

TIMELINE

Year	Event
1956	Born on 29 September in Chiswick, London.
1968	Moves to Sheffield.
1968	Olympic Games, Mexico.
	At the age of twelve, watches the Olympics on TV and queues up in Sheffield to watch John and Sheila Sherwood as they walk past with their Olympic medals.
	Joins Hallamshire Harriers and becomes a middle-distance specialist.
1970	Sheila Sherwood gives Seb his first pair of running shoes. He takes them to an English schools track championships.
	Seb's father, Peter Coe, becomes his coach.

1972   Runs first race against Steve Ovett in a schools cross-country event. Neither wins.

1974   Studies economics and social history at Loughborough University.

1977   Represents Loughborough University.

Wins 800m at the European Indoor Championships in San Sebastian, Spain.

Wins Emsley Carr Mile (3:57.67).

1978   Runs in the European Championships, Prague. Finishes third in the 800m.

1979   Sets two world records in Oslo, Norway: 800m (1:42.33) and one mile (3:48.95).

Sets a world record in Zürich, Switzerland: 1500m (3:32.03).

Voted 'Athlete of the Year' by *Track and Field News* for the first time.

Wins 'Sports Personality of the Year'.

1980   Olympic Games, Moscow:

800m – silver medal.

1500m – gold medal.

Sets new world record for 1000m (2:13.40).

1981   Beats own world record for 1000m (2:12.18). Stands for the next eighteen years.

Beats world record for fastest mile twice: in Zürich (3:48.53) and in Brussels (3:47.33).

Beats 800m record in Florence (1:41.73),

Remains unbeaten until August 1997, by Wilson Kipketer.

Voted 'Athlete of the Year' by *Track and Field News* for the second time.

1982   With Peter Elliott, Gary Cook and Steve Cram, sets a world record for the 4 x 800m (7:03.89). The record remains unbeaten for twenty-four years.

European Championships, Athens: 800m – silver medal.

Appointed Member of the Order of the British Empire (MBE).

1983   Breaks own indoor record in the 800m (1:44.91), in Cosford, England.

Breaks own world record in the 1000m (2:18.58), in Oslo, Norway.

Wins Emsley Carr Mile for the second time (4:03.37).

1984   Olympic Games, Los Angeles:

800m – silver medal.

1500m – gold medal. Sets a new Olympic record (3:32.53). The only person ever to win the 1500m title back-to-back in the Olympic Games.

1986   European Championships, Stuttgart. 800m – gold medal. 1500m – silver medal.

1500m personal best (3:29.77) in Rieti, Italy.

Only the fourth man in history to break 3:30.00 for the 1500m.

1988   Denied the chance to defend title at the 1988 Olympic Games in Seoul. The *Daily Mirror*'s 'Coe Must Go' campaign.

1990   Retires from competitive athletics.
        Appointed Officer of the Order of the British Empire (OBE).

1992   Elected MP for Falmouth and Camborne, for the Conservative Party.

1997   Loses seat in the general election.
        Becomes William Hague's chief of staff.

2000   Created a life peer, as Baron Coe of Ranmore, Surrey.

2003   Elected to the board of the IAAF (International Association of Athletics Federations)

2004   Barbara Cassani resigns and Seb becomes Chairman of the Olympic bid.

2005   Presentation to the IOC results in London being selected as the host city for 2012 Olympic Games.

2006   Given a special award at the BBC Sports Personality of the Year ceremony.
        Appointed a Knight Commander of the Order of the British Empire (KBE).

2007   Elected Vice-president of the International

Association of Athletics Federations.

2008   Father and coach, Peter Coe, dies on 9 August on the eve of the Beijing Olympics. He was eighty-eight.

2012   London scheduled to host the thirtieth summer Olympic Games.

INDEX

Note: SC denotes Sebastian Coe. Page numbers in italic denote entries in the Timeline section. Due to its ubiquity, entries may be assumed to refer to business unless otherwise indicated.

HOW TO BUILD A GREAT BUSINESS IN TOUGH TIMES

WILL KING

Starting a business in these recessionary times might seem like a busted flush but entrepreneur Will King firmly believes there is no time like the present. Using redundancy as his springboard, Will started his über-cool brand King of Shaves in the eye of the last recession. Will's belief is that if you can create a business that survives in a downturn, it will prosper when the good times return. After all, the ability to bootstrap in the early days is a critical part of starting any business.

Will King is full of great ideas and will share with you the best of them. Never one to follow market conventions, Will shows you how to 'zag' while your competitors 'zig' and reveals his SPACE philosophy – a powerful code for disrupting the market and being successful. King of Shaves has won numerous awards including Company of the Year 2008 and Product Business of the Year 2009. Will's ambition and enthusiasm are infectious and are combined with clear and compelling insights on how to make your business dreams a reality, regardless of what the markets are doing.

NON-FICTION / BUSINESS 978 0 7553 1999 2

THE 80 MINUTE MBA

RICHARD REEVES AND JOHN KNELL

Think of *The 80 Minute MBA* as your reduced Shakespeare for business. A traditional MBA might get you in the door, but it won't help you much once you are in. *The 80 Minute MBA* is for anyone in business who wants to get ahead without going back to school. A formal business education is great for anyone who wants to think in the same straight lines as the next person, but what if you want inspiration, creative thinking and a set of dynamic approaches in less time than it takes most meetings to get past coffee and biscuits?

Richard Reeves and John Knell have sorted the great business ideas and key issues from the rest, so you don't have to. They cover all the crucial topics including leadership, sustainability and ethics, community-building, corporate culture and finance – delivered in a way that will really make you sit up and think.

The 80 Minute MBA will wake up your mind with fresh ideas and save you a bundle on getting ahead in business.

NON-FICTION / BUSINESS 978 0 7553 1890 2

Coming soon from Business Plus:

On the Brink *Hank Paulson* £18.99
A fast-paced and dramatic re-telling of the financial crisis that nearly bought the developed world to its knees. Hank Paulson was at the absolute epicentre of the recent economic storm, and his account of how he dealt with the greatest financial crisis since the Great Depression will make for absolutely fascinating reading.

One Minute Entrepreneur *Ken Blanchard,* £8.99
Don Hutson, Ethan Willis
Multi-million copy selling author Ken Blanchard returns with much-needed advice on how to create and sustain a successful business.

Work Less, Achieve More *Fergus O'Connell* £12.99
Shows you how to move from a situation where you feel stressed and out of control at work to one where you feel satisfied with a good, solid week, having met all your targets and ready to go home with the confidence of a job well done.

The Flipside *Adam J. Jackson* £7.99
A setback can change the course of your life. But why should the change be a negative one? The flipside is the hidden opportunity inside each problem that this book helps you find to turn failure into success. Full of life-affirming stories, *The Flipside* will change the way you look at adversity, and help you turn setbacks into new chances.

Globality *Sirkin, Hemerling and* £9.99
Bhattacharya
Globality describes a world where new companies in emerging markets such as China, India, Brazil and Russia can compete with, and win business from, the established players in the West, and identifies what the threats and opportunities are.

Know Me, Like Me, Follow Me *Penny and Thomas Power* £9.99
Guide to understanding the online environment from expert author who created Ecademy, the world's first online business network.